James Withey is the founder of The Recovery Letters, a project that publishes online letters from people recovering from depression. He is the co-editor of the bestselling book *The Recovery Letters: Addressed to People Experiencing Depression.*

James trained as a person-centred counsellor and worked in addiction, homelessness and mental health services for fifteen years. He lives with depression and writes and speaks about mental health.

Twitter: @RecoveryLetters and @jameswwithey

How To Tell Depression to Piss Off

40 Ways to Get Your Life Back

A How To Book

James Withey

ROBINSON

ROBINSON

First published in Great Britain in 2020 by Robinson

1 3 5 7 9 10 8 6 4 2

A CIP catalogue record for this book
is available from the British Library.

ISBN: 978-1-47214-452-2

Typeset in Sentinel by Initial Typesetting Services, Edinburgh
Printed and bound in Great Britain by Clays Ltd, Elcograf S.p.A.

Papers used by Robinson are from well-managed forests and other responsible sources.

Robinson
An imprint of
Little, Brown Book Group
Carmelite House
50 Victoria Embankment
London EC4Y 0DZ

An Hachette UK Company
www.hachette.co.uk

www.littlebrown.co.uk

How To Books are published by Robinson, an imprint of
Little, Brown Book Group. We welcome proposals from
authors who have first-hand experience of their subjects.
Please set out the aims of your book, its target market
and its suggested contents in an email to
howto@littlebrown.co.uk

For Mum, Dad, Rach and Lou

Contents

Introduction   9

1   Get help when you don't feel like getting help   13
2   Don't listen to the lies   19
3   Do the opposite   23
4   Acceptance. You can't fight with ghosts   27
5   You're unwell, not crazy   31
6   But there's really nothing wrong with being crazy   34
7   Be nice to yourself (because depression won't)   38
8   Punch your cuckoo   42
9   Whose voice is it anyway?   45
10 Get humble   48
11 Talk, talk, talk (and then talk some more)   51
12 Get angry. Very, very angry   56
13 I'm all right. I'm okay   59
14 Finding your strong bits   62
15 I miss being me – getting over me-phobia   66
16 Celebrate small steps (they're actually huge)   70

17 Get some sleep   75
18 Read some stories   78
19 Depression? You're having a laugh, aren't you?   81
20 Second by second – not day by day   84
21 Do the work when you're well   87
22 Intrude on the intrusive thoughts   91
23 Be, like, totally nice to others   96
24 Get your identity tags   99
25 There are many other crazies out there   103
26 Cut down on the booze   106
27 Get a hobby – get a toolbox   110
28 It's okay if depression sometimes wins   115
29 This is your early warning call   117
30 Ditch your crap friends   120
31 Yeah, cheers, thanks a lot   125
32 Medicate! Medicate!   129
33 Rest   135
34 Slides and ladders   138
35 Finding the point in 'What's the bloody point?'   142
36 Start sharing   145
37 Download some hope   149
38 Get better painkillers and do mindfulness your way   154
39 Darken your humour (mwah ha ha)   160
40 Take pride in staying alive   163

    Afterword by Dr Ben Janaway   167

Introduction

Depression is a git. Truly it is.

It's an illness that constantly tries to take you down; that belittles you, criticises you, blames you, that gives you unbearable pain, drains you of your motivation and concentration, creates sleepless nights, anger, memory loss and has the capacity to kill you. It needs to be given a darn good seeing to. I'm being polite; it needs a good beating at the very least.

When I was first unwell with depression, I was desperate to know what to *do*. What action should I take? What should I be saying to myself? How do I manage something that feels utterly unmanageable?

This book gives you forty ways to get to a better place with this terrible illness. It gives you ideas and techniques to tackle depression. Unfortunately, we can't always get it to go away completely, but these tips will help you prioritise *you* and not the illness.

These strategies are born out of my own discovery of

what works to manage depression, which I still live with, as well as from many years working professionally with people with depression. I have been on both sides and know how destructive this illness is, but I also know how resilient we can be.

Depression hasn't beaten me because I keep throwing everything at it. Every time I think I've beaten depression, I haven't. But every time I think depression has beaten me, it hasn't. Yes, it's exhausting, but continuing to fight means we get moments in our lives that are wonderful, and those moments are worth every ounce of effort. And, crucially, depression doesn't win.

I'm definitely not saying, 'Ohhh, look at me! I'm all cured from depression and everything.' Because I'm not. Far from it. I know depression's not going to leave completely, but at the same time, I'm not going to let it win.

You don't need to read this book in order; dip in and out if you like. Also there's no hurry to read it all in one sitting: just go slowly and gently. It's fine not to like or agree with all forty ways, and you don't need to do them all at the same time – frankly it would be exhausting if you did. No matter what stage of depression you are at, there will be methods that can help. You might have just been diagnosed, be in the middle of a horrendous acute phase or recovering.

Pick the methods that appeal to you and give them a go. Then give them another go. Depression is a pernicious bugger, so you have to keep trying. Imagine it as bindweed trying to strangle a plant; you have to keep hacking away to keep it at bay.

Keep going, and, by the way, you're doing really great.

James

11

1. Get help when you don't feel like getting help

13

Great news! Your solicitor has just phoned. You've unexpectedly inherited a 14-foot crocodile. It turns out he's nasty, he bites, he needs constant attention, he takes up a huge amount of space, he keeps you awake, you don't know how to look after crocodiles and he's going to be around for a while. You live alone. What do you do?

You get some help, pronto.

The problem is you feel you shouldn't need help with the crocodile. I mean, other people easily manage their huge, vicious animals, don't they? Also you're ashamed that you have a crocodile living with you in the first place; how do you tell the neighbours?

Let's say this again. You need help. You ain't going to be able to manage this croc alone.

Asking for help with depression is hard because you may feel ashamed admitting there's something wrong with your mind, because this means that there's something wrong with *you*. It means that you're not strong enough to make it go away. It means you aren't capable of sorting it out by yourself.

Depression yells at you and says that you're not worthy of getting help. Why would anyone want to help *you*? Who would spend time helping *you*? There are so many *other* people in greater need. They should get the help instead. At first it can seem easier to be 'strong' and withhold what we're feeling. Carry on and keep it all inside. For too long we have championed the quality of reticence, but real strength lies in vulnerability. Admitting you need help and proactively asking for it takes real guts. Strength is saying, 'I'm scared.' Strength is saying, 'I don't know what these feelings are.' Strength is saying, 'I don't know what's wrong with me. I need help.' Strength is saying, 'It feels like something is taking over me and I don't know what to do.'

If we admit we need help, then we're accused of not having enough resilience, of being a weak, insipid, broken snowflake. Then, of course, others trivialising mental health with 'cures' doesn't help things. We're still told that depression can be sorted out by simply pulling our trousers up, or eating four mangos a day, or increasing our chia seed intake to 360 grams. FYI, I've tried all of these and you end up farting with a wedgie.

Before you get to the stage where you can reach out for help, you will need to do the following:

1. Challenge your own shame
2. Challenge society's stigma
3. Challenge depression's voice

Without taking these steps, you won't pick up the phone and get the help you need. These doubts will block your way and hold you in a nasty limbo. The work here is to do a bit of rethinking and ask yourself 'Why would I not be worthy of help?' 'Is there anything different or special about me that means I am not deserving of some support?' Let me butt in and answer these questions. You aren't special (sorry about that) – you do need help and you are worthy of help. I'll say that again:

YOU ARE WORTHY OF HELP.

(I've written that in a huge font so it means it's important.)

It can be easy to get someone else to arrange the help you need, but – and you're not going to like this – please do this yourself. By all means, have people alongside you, supporting you, finding phone numbers, recommending websites and services, but you make the actual call yourself. It's important to accept your illness and be responsible for it. I realise I now sound like my old secondary-school headmaster, Mr McRoberts, so I won't labour the point.

Once you have decided you need help, it can be daunting to know where to start. What worked for me, and many others I've spoken to, is to have a team on hand. A group of loved ones, or support workers, in whatever form, to champion you as you seek help.

Maybe someone can do the initial search for support groups for you, or walk with you to your first doctor or psychiatric appointment (and take you out for gooey cake afterwards), or just be in the room when you make a call to a mental health charity for more advice. Or you can go out for a meal after your first counselling appointment. Or be whisked away to Venice for the evening on a private jet, for a night of crispy artichoke hearts with creamy bagna cauda and some organic Prosecco from the Conegliano Valdobbiadene region, all set amongst the golden lights of the Rialto Bridge, the quiet lapping waves of the Grand Canal and the almost silent passing of a gondola . . . If you have friends like that, please introduce me.

If you don't have friends with private jets (where did we all go wrong?) and just have bloody awful depression, then it's a good idea to tell your team what they can do to help, because people will ask.

17

Texts are really important. Explain that you may not always reply to them, but will always appreciate them. Texts without direct questions work the best. So 'Thinking of you' is generally better than 'How are you?' because it places less pressure on you to respond. Trying to articulate how you feel other than saying, 'I feel shit,' or 'I feel nothing,' is really hard when in the depths of depression. Jokes are good too, or sending a YouTube video of funny chickens or a picture of a cat with a Santa hat.

Tell people you might cancel plans at the last minute. Once I arranged with friends to come down for the day, but when they got here I couldn't see them – I was too ill – so they went back home. I felt awful but relieved and was so grateful for their understanding. It's good to explain to people that this might happen and that you'll need some flexibility with arrangements. Or you could plan a meeting but make it short – meet for lunch for an hour, or a brief coffee but not a whole weekend away to Barcelona.

The tendency with depression is to withdraw from people we love because we're ashamed of what depression has done to us and because we feel we can't manage.

Remember, we need help with that blasted crocodile, which means trying to tell people what we need, despite feeling unworthy.

2. Don't listen to the lies

We all tell lies, right?

Admittedly, not always massive ones like 'My ginger chihuahua won an Oscar six times in a row,' or 'I'm actually an undercover Ukrainian astronaut,' but gentle lies that serve to protect ourselves or someone else. 'No, honestly, I really didn't get your message,' or even 'I don't watch television at all. I'd rather meditate all evening sipping a bowl of clear soup.'

Depression is the worst liar in the world, like ever, ever. Ever.

Depression is really convincing – the best con artist you'll ever comes across. Those guys shuffling cups and balls on the street are nothing in comparison. Those spam e-mails that promise you a tax rebate? Dirt in the street when matched with depression. Those pyramid schemes that promise you an annual income of £350,000? Depression beats them hands down.

Lies that depression tells us include:

- You are never going to get better.
- You are a worthless piece of hairy hog rump.
- Other people might get better but you're different (and weird and ugly).
- Being unwell is all your fault.
- The world is a shitty, shitty, shitty place.
- You will never be able to manage this pain. Give up now.
- All your loved ones think you're a burden and smell of poo.

Any of these sound familiar? Depression screams these lies in the loudest, most vile voice possible, whilst also prodding you with a red-hot poker. Quite the combination.

I had a friend at school who told the most fantastic lies. The first few lies I bought into, but then they became more outlandish and I strongly suspected he wasn't telling the truth. After the ninth ridiculous lie, I saw him for what he was: a liar, and a really bad one at that. He said his dad was the head of the Royal Navy, that his aunt was making films in Hollywood and that when he was eighteen he would inherit a fortune from his grandfather, who made famous sweets. What rank was his father in the Royal Navy, I asked. 'Lieutenant captain commander colonel' was all he could come up with. What films had his aunt been in? 'Ones with Marilyn Monroe,' he said (she was long since dead). What sweets did his grandfather make? Apparently, some diamond-shaped ones called 'Choccy Lovelies'. Now, you can try to bamboozle an eleven-year-old boy with dead Hollywood film stars and made up naval rankings, but I knew my sweets, and Choccy Lovelies definitely did not exist. He was a compulsive liar, but his bold-faced lies pale in comparison to depression's continual disgusting drip-drip of lies.

What makes depression's falsehoods so bad is that it's incredibly hard to challenge these lies, or even believe that they are lies at all. It is crucial to realise how much the illness deceives and to acknowledge the power of the lies it tells us. It's like my school friend: he seemed convincing at first, but when I started digging around and asked questions it all fell apart.

Try it with depression. Why would you be the most despicable person on the planet? Is it really completely true that all your loved ones hate having you around as you're such a nuisance? Is there really no hope at all? Put depression on a lie detector test from one of those daytime talk shows and the graph would be leaping up and down faster than a cocaine-fuelled jumping bean.

Spend some time writing the kind of lies that depression tells you on a piece of paper and then write in big capital letters:

THESE ARE LIES, LIES, LIES!

21

Preferably in a red pen with a picture of some pants on fire.

I have my list on my fridge, and when depression starts screaming at me, I look at it and remind myself of the lies.

Remember that what you're feeling inside your mind is depression telling you lies.

3. Do the opposite

Depression is really good at getting you to stay exactly   23
where you are – in a dirty bed, without showering for days,
not even bothering to get up and make a cheese sandwich.
You can spend weeks not seeing other people, not getting
any fresh air and cursing at anything remotely cheerful.
The cheeping birds and the excited barking dogs are there
simply to annoy you. The smiling woman in the petrol
station is part of a conspiracy to irritate you as much as
possible.

The trick to combatting depression, at any stage of the
illness, is to try to **do the opposite of what depression
is telling you to do.** Now, this is not easy. In fact, it's
really, really hard, but the effort alone counts for a huge
amount.

This means having some food when eating seems
pointless, phoning a friend when you don't want to talk
to anyone, going to the shops when stepping outside is
terrifying.

And it's okay if you don't complete the whole task. Maybe you have a cheese sandwich but don't eat the whole thing. Maybe you send a text rather than phone your friend. Maybe you get half way to the shops and come back. Even small things – like dusting a coffee table, reading a magazine, walking around the park – count, if depression is telling you not to do it.

The act of disobedience is the key here. It's time for some anarchy! I do love a bit of anarchy and it's time to rebel against depression.

When you do manage to do the opposite, it feels really good. This is because depression is corrosive and never has your best interests at heart. The opposite is always going to be better for you.

One day, it took me seven hours to plant a shrub in my garden. Honestly. The conversation in my head with depression went like this:

> ME: I really need to plant the shrub today, otherwise the roots may not take.
>
> DEPRESSION: Don't bother.
>
> ME: But I do need to do it today.
>
> DEPRESSION: If you plant it, it probably won't grow anyway.
>
> ME: I want to plant it. It would feel like an achievement.

I need to do something today. The plant needs to go in the ground.

DEPRESSION: Stay in bed, wallow and think dark thoughts.

ME: Okay.

DEPRESSION: You're rubbish at gardening anyway.

ME: That's true.

A few hours passed, depression had me in its grip, but I wanted to plant that shrub. Small steps, I told myself, small steps. From my bedroom to the garden is not very far, so thankfully it was literally small steps. I got to the kitchen, sat down, had some coffee. More time passed. Then I opened the kitchen door and felt the air. More time passed. I put my shoes on, which always feels like a huge effort, and went outside. I sat at the garden table. More time passed. The light was fading. I finally got the shrub, got a spade, but then had to sit down again. Depression started shouting.

DEPRESSION: You can't dig holes. You'll kill the plant. You're rubbish.

I turned into a three-year-old having a tantrum.

ME: I hate you. You're horrible and vile and I hate, hate, hate you!

More time passed. I went back inside. I got some more coffee. I watched some television and went out into the garden again, gritting my teeth. I dug a hole, put the shrub in, gave it some water and went back to bed.

> DEPRESSION: That took you a long time. You're so hopeless. The shrub is lopsided, and it won't grow where you've planted it.

> ME: But I did it. That what counts. And, more importantly, I didn't bloody listen to you.

Oh, and the shrub is alive and well and blooms every summer. Take that, depression.

4. Acceptance. You can't fight with ghosts

27

I can't do maths. I mean, I'm really bad at it. I don't bother looking at my change when I leave a shop because I won't know if it's correct or not. At work, the calculator is minimised on my computer in case of mental arithmetic emergencies. And don't get me started on fractions, division or those bloody isosceles triangles. I am 450 per cent rubbish. I accept it. I can't do maths.

When I was first unwell with depression, I was so angry with myself for being ill I was determined to get completely better. I would work my arse off to get rid of depression and ensure that it never, ever came back. I tried everything. Gardening, meditation, cycling, self-help groups, creative writing, retreats, pottery. If I had been offered baby-lizard cuddling, I would have tried it. Actually, baby-lizard cuddling sounds really great, doesn't it?

I couldn't accept that depression was going to be part of my life. I wanted myself back. I wanted the guy that could laugh uncontrollably and not hide from people I knew in the cereal aisle of the supermarket. I wanted the 'me' back that didn't want to jump in front of trains. I wanted the 'me' back that could hold down a full-time job and not feel that brushing my teeth was a Herculean task. Depression had crushed me, and I was seriously pissed off.

Maybe I just wasn't trying hard enough? There had to be something I hadn't tried to make it go away completely. There had to be a pill I hadn't taken or a book I hadn't read or an app that I could download that would cure me.

After many years of ridiculous fighting (and making my depression much worse), I came to accept that depression was going to be with me for the rest of my life. I went and told my psychiatrist.

> PSYCH: Yes, I think you're right. You need to treat your depression like asthma.
>
> ME: What? Will I need some sort of inhaler? Should I dust the house more?
>
> PSYCH: Well, you probably do need to dust the house more, but no, that's not what I mean. Treat it like a chronic illness. Something that you have to manage rather than overcome. Something that's going to be with you for the rest of your life in some form.

He was right. Accepting depression stops you needlessly fighting. It's like throwing your best punches into a ghost who just looks back at you with disdain, smoking a cigarette, raising his eyes to heaven, completely unharmed. It's utterly pointless.

Depression is so exhausting; it requires so much to get through the day. You need all the energy and rest you can get. Let's hope it won't always be with you, but accepting that it *is* with you now is really important and conserves your energy for managing the illness, day by day.

Accepting depression also helps you roll with the ups and downs of depression, though sometimes it feels like the downs and downs of depression. (Depression would be a rubbish rollercoaster.) Once you start letting go of the need to heal completely, the need to rid yourself of depression altogether, it starts to get slightly easier.

Accepting that depression is in my life is probably the most effective thing I do, day to day, to keep depression in check. It doesn't mean I've given in, but I do have to acknowledge that it's with me. Accepting depression doesn't mean that I'm weak, and it doesn't mean that things can't improve. It simply says, it's with me and I acknowledge that.

Remember, don't fight with ghosts.

5. You're unwell, not crazy

I am completely bonkers.

I should be in a white restraint suit, banging my head against a padded cell, only being let out to have my head shaved and eat a bowl of Oliver Twist-like gruel. I am one of those people you see in Victorian paintings with crazed eyes and their tongue lolling about like a dead haddock. I should be committed to a nineteenth-century asylum, where I spend the day screaming through the bars of my cell and writing indecipherable messages on the walls in my own blood.

Nothing is the same; my perception is like a goldfish in a small, thick bowl; I can't concentrate; my memory is terrible; time seems to pass in long, dolloping seconds or speeds up like a gazelle fleeing a ravenous lion on the Serengeti. I seem to be existing in a world that isn't like everyone else's.

This is depression. Great isn't it? What good is a holiday in the Seychelles or the smell of freshly buttered toast on a

Sunday morning when you can end up feeling like a liquid-ised jellyfish

So, for the record, you're unwell; and remember that we know depression lies. You haven't accidently slipped into a vortex of derangement, nor have pixies injected your brain with a hefty dose of delirium. You're unwell.

Let's say that again: you're unwell, you're unwell, you're unwell. I'm slapping you in the face (in a nice, loving way, obviously) and saying it again: you're unwell. Is it going in? No? Well, let's say it again. You're unwell.

This isn't a character flaw.

It hasn't happened because you haven't been good enough or kind enough or not given enough money to the local deprived alpacas charity. This isn't your fault.

Telling yourself you're unwell will help put into context the world you've found yourself in and legitimatise the feelings you're having. Some people may not class depression as a proper illness, but they're officially idiots who wouldn't manage thirty seconds of depression. Please don't listen to them; they're numbskulls, and no one wants to play with them in the playground. Listen to me instead. Listen to all the experts around the world.

You have to keep telling yourself you're unwell, other-wise the blame game will take over. The Blame Game™ is a hideous board game for one player that's played in your head, where you blame yourself constantly for everything, all the time. The rules basically consist of saying lots of 'should's. I should have been stronger; I should have seen it coming; I should be able to shake myself out of it; I should get a grip.

The Blame Game is not a good one for Christmas afternoon with the in-laws. Depression *loves* The Blame Game, by the way – thrives on it – and unless you teach yourself how to win, then depression will always take home the trophy. It will dance around the room in green tartan hot pants, shouting, 'Woohoo! I won! You lost, you massive looooser! Loooser.' Frankly, you don't want to see this. No one wants to see this.

The first move in winning The Blame Game is to keep telling yourself you're unwell. So, again, say it again, all together now ...

6. But there's really nothing wrong with being crazy

The thing is, who wants to be normal anyway?

Okay, so admittedly, sometimes when my depression is at peak weirdness, I long to be Ian, a civil servant from Hemel Hempstead, who comes home each night to a well-ordered life, where the dog hasn't eaten the kitchen roll, there isn't a leak in the toilet or a dead bird in the chimney breast, and who has no intrusive thoughts telling him he should jump out of an eighteenth-floor window. His plants stay alive, his carpets stay clean and his Sellotape never does that annoying thing where you can't find the end.

But, increasingly, I've come to understand that the part of me that's susceptible to depression is actually quite interesting and makes me *me*. And it probably makes me more interesting than Ian.

Here's a conversation I had with my husband:

ME: Can I get, like, a brain transplant or something?

HUSBAND: No, absolutely not. Mostly because there is no such thing.

ME: Or a lobotomy?

HUSBAND: No, because this isn't 1947.

ME: Is there an exchange programme where I can have a new brain for a few days a week when I'm feeling crap and then give it back?

HUSBAND: Do I really have to answer these questions?

ME: Well, someone should have invented these things. I blame the person who hasn't invented brain swapping.

The trouble is you're stuck with yourself. You can't swap your brain with your neighbour who is always smiling, jogging, sipping home-made oat-and-bulgar-wheat smoothies and joyously singing Broadway show tunes as they head out each morning. They are definitely not awake at 3.30 a.m., eating cake from the fridge with a teaspoon, wondering when the pain will end.

For years I loathed my ability to empathise WITH EVERY LITTLE BLOODY THING. If I accidently killed an ant I would spend hours ruminating about how the mother ant would be looking for her child; and when she found him dead would be inconsolable and throw herself into a pond, leaving all her other baby ants motherless; and then they would all throw themselves into the pond as well because of the grief; and then, when the rest of the ant colony finds the baby ants dead in the pond, they would also lose the will to live and throw themselves into the pond too. I would then feel responsible for killing hundreds, thousands, possibly millions of ants. This would, in turn, wreck the ecosystem of the whole world and everyone would die.

I always feel too much. I'm basically an anti-psychopath. Increasingly though, I've realised the only way to manage feeling all this weird stuff is to embrace it and not crave to be Ian from Hemel Hempstead. Because Ian doesn't have the intuition that I have; he doesn't feel the joy in things in the same way that I do. Plus he has really boring socks.

When joy does come into my life, I feel it more keenly. Seeing hundreds of starlings swooping across the sky will make me smile more than Ian, who is looking at his map and tutting. Observing someone singing as they walk, lost in their own world of music, is a privilege to me, whereas Ian is just annoyed at them as they've got in his way. When yellow leaves fall around my feet and I try to catch one, it's a moment of pure childish glee, but Ian is on the phone to the council to get the leaves cleaned up.

Yes, we may feel more crappy stuff, but when we feel

more joy, it's spectacularly beautiful, and that's much, much better than not feeling it at all.

Oh, and go and buy some completely weird socks. Trust me, it really helps.

7. Be nice to yourself (because depression won't)

You're sat on one side of a large set of scales. Depression is on the other side. At the moment you're high in the sky because depression is heavy, powerful and stubborn. It's also sticking it's tongue out at you. Nice.

We need to level the scales out, to add things that comfort you and that depression will hate. You won't feel like treating yourself well because, as we know, depression is telling you you're worthless, but give it a go.

Get some nice food in. Choose some treats that will comfort you and some food that is good for you, preferably both at the same time. If you can afford to, spend a little extra on some quality grub that will properly nourish you. Order your weekly food shop to be delivered to your door; no one likes to deal with supermarkets in person. You also have my full permission to add in something indulgent every so often. I know, generous of me, eh? So the odd chocolate bar, cheesecake, ginger biscuits or microwave chicken jalfrezi is all good.

The scales are starting to tip a little.

Change your bed sheets and duvet. We all should do that more anyway (okay, *I* should do this more often), but with depression this matters more, especially as we spend more time in bed with this illness. If you only have energy for one task, choose this one. There's nothing quite like the feel and smell of clean sheets when you go to bed. If you're able to hang your sheets to dry outside, even better, as you get that nice fresh-air smell. And get some new bed linen if you can: something soothing and cheering. It's fine to have scenes from Winnie-the-Pooh eating honey or Homer Simpson eating a burger on your duvet cover. Also invest in a great blanket for winter – one that can wrap around you whilst you watch old films on the television and sip hot chocolate. You can also create a dart board representing depression and throw your unwanted marshmallows at it.

Self-care is admittedly easy to say and hard to do. It doesn't mean that you have to have a pedicure every other day or buy a crate of those really expensive smelly candles. Although if you want to spend money on something that smells of toilet cleaner, then go for it. Self-care is not just about treats and comfort but also about conserving and managing your energy so you can deal with depression.

This means saying no to stuff and knowing when doing too much is going to make your depression worse.

'Depression is so selfish.' I once heard someone on the train say to their friend when a person had tragically taken their own life on the railway tracks. They were complaining about the massive inconvenience of being ten minutes late for their very, very important meeting with very, very, very important people. 'So many people are worse off than them. They should be grateful they're not living in Bangladesh, living on scraps of food. Then they wouldn't be depressed, would they?'

My desire to throw my banana yoghurt drink in their face was strong. But I really like banana yoghurt drinks, it's one of my comfort drinks, so I restrained myself. Plus, if I had thrown it in their face, I would instantly have regretted it and felt compelled to lick it off, and some people don't like that.

Being ill with depression is not selfish. In fact, those of us with it are much more likely to spend our time thinking of others and putting them before ourselves, which can contribute to our depression in the first place. With this illness, we have to learn to think, feel and look after ourselves. If it were selfish to have depression, our self-care would always be to the exclusion of others, which it isn't. So there.

To be fair, depression will definitely make you think about yourself. It will make you think that you are the most vile, most revolting, most shameful, most disgusting human that ever existed in the world ever. But that's not going to help you manage your depression. Think for a moment how self-critical we are with depression. Where does it get us? A big fat nowhere. More unwell. More depressed. More self-loathing.

During one particular week, when my depression was particularly awful, I agreed to have friends stay overnight, give two book talks, travel four hours to see a relative and go to work as normal. The next week my depression got a lot uglier, and I ended up in hospital. You would think after that I would've learnt to take things easier and manage things better, but denial is a big part of depression, and I convinced myself that I could still do all the things I used to do and not get ill. It took me many more months, more crisis points, lots of psychiatric visits and one twisted ankle to admit things had to change and I needed to take better care of myself.

Don't be like me; flies that can't escape out of the window learn faster than me. Be nice to yourself. And buy more yoghurt drinks.

8. Punch your cuckoo

My depression is a cuckoo.

Yep, it's one of those brutish, bully birds that takes over your nest when you're at your weakest, sets up home and breeds. It then convinces you it's your fault that it's taken over your nest, and makes you feel guilty and ashamed.

We need to try to kick the cuckoo out of the nest, or at least reclaim your own space in the nest, even if you might need to share it with the cuckoo.

When we imagine depression as something 'other', an external thing, it helps. Imagination is an incredibly powerful tool – as powerful as memory. When we apply our imagination to depression, it fixes an image into our head and externalises the illness.

It could be a cuckoo, but anything will work. Winston Churchill went for a black dog, which is unfair to black dogs, in my opinion, but whatever. I suppose cuckoos can't help it, but their manners leave a lot to be desired. It's like, dude, just build your own nest.

43

Don't go for an animal that you love; that really won't work. Or something really cute. You can't use a five-week-old puppy called 'Schmuggins' or a baby otter who waves at you from the river bank because, even though no animals are being harmed in this metaphor, you still need something that you don't have an emotional attachment with. So no baby pandas and or wide-eyed young giraffes.

My cuckoo is a bastard. He pecks me, sometimes all through the day and it hurts. He also berates me, shouts at me and spits. He's a delight. Sometimes I put up with him by ignoring him, pretending not to care and getting on with my day. I rise above his constant, ridiculous demands by going to work or watching television, and sometimes he gets bored and goes to sleep for a while.

Usually though, I punch him in the face. Don't be alarmed! As I've said, hitting birds in your mind is fine.

I smack him one, square in the beak, leaving it squashed and bent. And stars appear above his head like you see in cartoons. 'Take that you buggering stupid bird. You think you're going to get in my head today? Well, you're not.' Whack. 'Take that too, and nurse your injuries rather than pecking me. Not so cocky now, are you? Eh?' Thwack.

The anger and violence make me feel stronger. Again, don't worry, I don't hit cuckoos or any other birds, or anything else, in real life. Unless it's a seagull – those bastards just deserve it. I feel more in control; I feel I have more power, energy, and that I don't just exist as a punch bag for imaginary cuckoos.

Have a think about what your depression animal, bird, mythical creature or monster is. See it in your mind, give it a vile name if you want, and put on your boxing gloves.

9. Whose voice is it anyway?

You know that voice in your head that's abusing you, telling you you're worthless and that being ill is all your fault?
That's depression, the illness talking, not you.

   It pays to recognise its voice so that you know when it's
talking. I often get caught by surprise when my illness starts
shouting at me because it sounds exactly like my own inner
voice. It can take me a while to go, 'Oh, it's you again. I'd
hoped you'd gone, but here you are. I know it's you, disguising
yourself as me. I hear you. You massive, massive twat.'

   When we know depression's voice, and become familiar
with its trademark phrases and patterns, we're in a much
better position to deal with it. It's a bit like when you are
learning another language. At first it doesn't make sense.
But then, as you grow familiar with the language's words
and rhythms, you become more informed, and it gives you
the freedom and power to talk back. My French is terrible; I once got box seats at the Paris opera because I got
confused with 'very cheap' and 'very expensive'. Several

times I have asked for a quesadilla when I wanted the bill in Spain, and however much I try, I can't pronounce the number six in Polish. But I'm getting more fluent in depression. I know a lot of the words and intonation; I'm starting to understand it more, day by day.

We're often told to trust our instincts – that gut feeling we all get that guides us to make the right decisions. The problem is that depression steals our gut feeling as well, so that we can't trust our instincts. If we trusted our gut feeling with depression, it would be telling us to blame ourselves, shame ourselves and hurt ourselves.

Once we get used to recognising which voice is depression and which is ours, we can then listen to our own voice more and ignore, or swear at, depression's voice. It takes practice and it's not easy but it does help. At the start, all you can hear is depression's voice because it's shouting the loudest. But people who shout the loudest (pick a politician of your choice) are often the ones we shouldn't listen to, and the same is true of depression.

I always have to sit down and think, 'Is this me or is this depression talking?' Usually, there are recognisable patterns. For example, depression's voice is always critical, abusive and extreme. If I have the strong desire to do something irrational, then it's definitely depression talking. Or if I suddenly decide that I have to storm out of the flat, that's depression again.

If you've lived with depression for a long time, it can be a real struggle to find your own voice because you've got used to not hearing it. But it's there. The essence of you hasn't gone because you're unwell; it's just a bit harder to locate.

I promise, you're there underneath and your voice will come out.

47

10. Get humble

48 I'm having an inner toddler tantrum on the floor of my psychiatrist's waiting room. It's like my brain is on its back, screaming, crying and will most likely go into a full-blown sulk afterwards. The receptionist, who is no doubt trained to look for inner tantrums, looks at me and smiles, and I somehow manage a smile back. She goes back to her typing and I go back to my tantrum.

In my head I'm ranting. 'All this totally sucks, big time. Why has depression picked on me? Why me? Why me? Why not the horrible man in the newsagent who always glares at me as if I'm stealing all the chocolate bars? Why not the nasty woman who knocked me down the stairs at the train station? Why not all of the other people who have been horrid to me over the years for no reason? Let them have depression instead. I can happily choose at least fifty people I know who deserve depression more than me.

'I mean, I try my hardest to be nice to people. I pay my taxes, I recycle, I run after people down the street when they've dropped their glasses. I'm very much against being horrible and tend to be very positive about cute fluffy kittens. So why do I have this crippling depression? Why punish me when I work hard and do my best?'

This is a great conversation to have with yourself that can go on for years and years. And it gets you absolutely nowhere. Actually, that's not completely true; it does get you angrier and angrier, and progressively more bitter and resentful – so that's something. The trouble is, I was asking myself the wrong questions. The better question is:

Why *shouldn't* it happen to me?

Or

Why *not* me?

And when we ask these questions, our humility starts to kick in, rather than our ego. (Did I sound a bit like Freud then? Excellent, that will boost my ego.) There's no reason why we shouldn't have depression; lots of other people do. It's awful, really awful, but there's no reason we should be exempt from it.

Illness is rubbish. It's a fact of life that we know about, but no one prepares us for. Our loved ones get ill, the cat gets ill, the person on the television gets ill, we get ill. We need lessons at school about illness because it always comes as a massive shock, rather than something we should expect to happen.

Being humble about depression is hard because it

involves accepting an illness that we hate. But knowing our limitations, what we can and can't control, will give you more energy for the fight against depression and looking after yourself.

Being humble is strength in my book because it makes us seek support and accept that we need to learn about the illness we've got. Being humble makes us realise that we're not perfect and the recovery journey won't be perfect either.

Let's all take a deep breath, admit we don't know everything, be open to change and new ideas, and keep going.

11. Talk, talk, talk (and then talk some more)

I know it's hard to talk. I know that you worry that if you do talk, you'll collapse even more than you have already. I know that you think if you do talk about depression, people will look at you as if you've turned into a stinking bottom boil, oozing green pus onto the street. But the thing about talking is that it helps.

There are many eminent psychiatrists, Ph.D.s and other people cleverer than me who can tell you the neuroscience and psychology of talking, but they will use words that even a decent spellchecker can't comprehend. As I'm a being with a simple brain, I think of it like this:

Get a pen and a piece of paper. No, actually go and get one; I promise this won't take long. Draw a picture of a person with a large body – this doesn't need to be anything Rembrandtesque, just a basic outline of a figure. You can add an unhappy mouth if you want, which is the universal sign for being depressed. Now, in the middle of the body draw lots of dark, intense, chaotic squiggles. That's depression, and that needs to come out. We can't pee or poo it out unfortunately, and we can't have it lanced like a boil, so the best way for it to come out is via your mouth. You could try spitting it out but that's just gross, so I would go for talking instead.

You know that person you've been friends with for ages that you don't have a lot in common with any more, who never talks about their feelings and the last time you saw them they seemed a little racist? DON'T TALK TO THEM. Find someone who isn't going to freak out when you say how you're feeling, who has always been a good listener and gives great hugs and free sweets. (The sweets part is really important.)

What you're looking for is a '4 a.m. person'. Someone who, in theory, wouldn't mind you calling them in the early hours if you really needed it. You're probably not going to actually do this, but it's that type of person you're looking for.

We don't all have these people in our lives, so helplines can be useful too. They help loads of people who are struggling just like you. For some, including me, the effort it takes to phone and talk to someone you don't know about your innermost feelings can be huge, so don't beat yourself up if this isn't the right support for you. Some of them do have a text service though, which you might find less daunting. It's the talking and offloading that counts.

Finding a good counsellor is a good idea. But you'll have to audition them. Not put them on a stage and get them to sing 'Memory' from Cats (although that would be entertaining); instead meet a lot of them before you find the right one for you. You may have no initial choice if you get allocated one for free through the health service, but that doesn't mean you can't ask to change to someone else if it doesn't work out. Ask questions, get a feel for who they are and if you can see yourselves working with them. There are lots of different types of counsellors and psychotherapists out there, using lots of different theory models, but the most crucial aspect is whether you feel able to open up and talk to them.

Private counsellors are expensive. Some have low-cost schemes or will reduce rates if you're not employed. They need to earn a living too, of course, but if you've had to make big financial changes in your life to accommodate depression, it can make private counselling impossible. For free counselling, you'll have to wait, and wait and wait. For my two lots of free counselling, I've waited

53

twenty-four months and eighteen months respectively, which is a heck of a long time when depression is stabbing you in the groin.

I've paid for private counselling and have been allocated people who couldn't cope with me talking about suicide, or we just didn't click for some reason, so private is not always better. But when it works, it's wonderful – often painful, but helpful, so it's worth the hunt for a good one, whether you're paying or not.

I've also had mental health workers talking a load of rubbish to me. One worker insisted that the only way my depression was going to be 'cured' was if I stayed in bed continuously for three weeks – no getting out at all. To be fair, I was allowed to go the toilet and make meals, but they were insistent that for the rest of the day and night I stayed in bed. When I came back to see them three weeks later, they were furious with me that I hadn't done what they said. It sounds unbelievable, but it's true, and mine is not the only ridiculous, medieval and frankly dangerous story like this. My point is: do some research for the right person and don't settle for anyone telling you jelly will cure depression, because it won't. Jelly is perfect for a trifle, so use it for that instead.

There are also peer support groups with whom you can talk. Again, you may need to audition them. I once went to a group which was a complete free-for-all. No one was facilitating the group, so some people spoke for forty minutes, taking up all the time whilst people tutted and sulked. If they're run well, these groups can really help because not only do you get to speak but also you get to listen too. You can gain a lot by hearing how other people manage their depression.

Finally, I'm absolutely not going to throw out the old, tired, clichéd phrase of 'A problem shared is a problem halved.' No wait – I am, because it's true.

12. Get angry. Very, very angry

If ever there was a time to swear, it's when you're ill with depression. If ever there was a time to get angry, it's now.

We're told anger is a bad thing. We're told that we should all feel calm and serene, like an organic tea bag gently dipping in and out of a warming cup of camomile tea. But I never feel calm when I think about depression. I feel terrible and angry. The more that people told me to love my depression, the more I hated it. And them.

'Think of it as a beautiful part of you, a lovely part of you that's just having a hard time,' one person said.

I tried. It didn't work.

'Imagine the darkness of depression is turning into a wondrous warming orb of love and light,' they said.

It didn't. It still felt cold and crappy and vile.

'Think of it as something crying and desperate that needs you to give it a big cuddle and some lovely comforting milk.'

I was happy to let it scream and die.

Depression doesn't love me, I don't love it. I accept it's there, but that doesn't mean I'm going to take it out to dinner at a fine-dining restaurant of its choice. So I got angry with depression.

'You are a bastard and I am NOT going to let you ruin my life,' I said.

Silence.

'You are a selfish, deplorable, attention-seeking, lying piece of smelly vomit.'

I felt stronger.

'If you think you're going to take me down, then you have another thing coming.'

I felt even better, like I had a small shield in my hands.

'You've done enough damage already. I've lost too much of my life. I'm going to fight for this. You aren't the boss of me!'

My anger at depression fuels me better than a bowl of porridge. It makes me keep fighting, hitting back, punching depression in the soft, ouchy parts. It doesn't eliminate depression altogether – if only it could – but it stands up to it and says I am not going to be bullied by it.

Bullies needs standing up to, they need confronting and to be told where to go. Ignoring them doesn't work, being nice and loving to them doesn't work; you need to get angry.

You have to play power games with depression. You

have to anticipate when it's going to attack and, if possible, get the first punch in. For example, some mornings I can feel my mood slipping; I've not fallen completely but I can feel my balance going. That's when I start to fight. I start talking back. I get angry. I force myself to get up and go to work, to go to the gym, to the shops, to do some gardening, whatever. I curse depression as I go. I can often be seen mumbling to myself, my eyes bulging, grinding my teeth.

What I'm saying is, 'Piss off, depression. Bugger off, sod off.' It keeps me walking. It keeps me going.

13. I'm all right. I'm okay.

ANNOYING MAN: Do you love yourself, James? I mean really, *really* love yourself?

I stared back at the man at the other side of the low coffee table with a vase of irritating plastic tulips in the middle.

ANNOYING MAN: Because only with self-love can we achieve our full potential. If you're ever going to move forward, you have to start to adore and cherish each and every part of yourself. Do you get it, hmm? Do you understand what I'm saying to you, James?'

I took a breath, then stood up and started pacing around the room.

ME: Love myself? Love myself? Are you freakin' kidding me? Are you on psychoactive drugs? Perhaps you've taken a draught of magic mushrooms? Every day I'm trying not to kill myself and you're telling me I need to love myself? How do I do that? Magic? Do you have a wand? Can you put a spell on me? Are you actually Dumbledore?

ANNOYING MAN: Who?

ME: Who? Who? Oh, for goodness sake!

There were two choices: I could either have poured the water in the vase over him or walked out. I remembered there was no water in the vase, so I walked out. Plus, if you don't know who Dumbledore is, I have no patience. Ex-twat-iarmus.

You simply can't go from hating your very existence to loving yourself in a few easy moves. It really doesn't work like that. And it especially doesn't work like that when you have depression.

When you see social media memes about how self-love will cure you of your depression, block that account. If someone tells you self-love is achievable by downloading their 30-minute app, ignore them. When someone takes you to one side and says self-love is achievable if you repeat 'I love you' every morning in a mirror for an hour, block them too. It's like saying to someone who has never been in the sea that they need to waterski one-legged across the Atlantic without falling over.

At the moment I don't want you to even try to say, 'I love myself'. DO NOT DO THAT because you will know how fake it is. It will feel superficial and flimsy, and devoid of anything that will nourish you. What we have to aim towards is thinking 'I'm all right.' Not 'I love myself with every fibre of my being.' Not 'I am a completely amazing, super talented, overtly beautiful, consummately creative, forever compassionate and, most of all, an utterly humble human being'. Just, 'I'm all right. I'm okay.'

61

I'm working on being all right with me. I'm never per-fect; I make tons of mistakes – I once mistook a plantain for a banana – but I'm okay. I'm not evil, I don't want to hurt anyone. I struggle with basic sudoku, but I think I'm all right.

The journey from 'I hate myself and want to die' to 'I'm all right. I'm okay' is admittedly long and hard, but that's just the aim – we don't need to get there on the express 62 bus. It's a case of each day trying to tell yourself you're okay and challenging what depression is telling you about yourself.

Remember, you're all right. You're okay.

14. Finding your strong bits

You can't brush your teeth, you can't get out of bed, you can barely talk and having a shower feels like something only other people do. Depression has wiped you out. It's won; you surrender. It's going to be like this forever, stuck in a filthy bed, with a filthy body and feeling like filth.

Except, there is always the word 'except'. Or 'but'. Actually, 'but' is a better word to use because it's funnier, because it sounds like a bottom. You need childish humour with depression – just work with me here.

I'm sat with a worker in a suicide respite centre I've come to stay in.

> ME: I'm annihilated. I'm obliterated. There's nothing of me left.
>
> WORKER: I don't think so.
>
> ME: And what do you know? Look at me. I'm a wreck. I can't stop crying. All I think about is suicide. Does that seem like a man who's got everything covered? Hmm?

WORKER: But you're still here.

ME: Here? But look where I am. In a suicide centre. Last night I wanted to kill myself. Not the height of togetherness. There are collapsible curtain poles in my bedroom, the knife drawer is locked in the kitchen and I haven't brought enough clean socks.

WORKER: But you're still here. You're still alive. That's amazing, James.

ME: What?

WORKER: You're still here. You're still alive. Despite all that's happened to you, all the pain that you're feeling, you're still here.

ME: Only because I can't think of an effective way to kill myself.

WORKER: But you're still here.

ME: Stop saying that.

WORKER: No, I won't. You are in the most agony a human can experience. You think you're worthless and unlovable. Depression has tried to take you down. But you're still here.

I looked at her. This woman who didn't know me until yesterday. I looked her in the eyes for the first time as I was crying. My glasses were all steamed up. There may have been some snot coming out of my nose, but let's gloss over that.

'But you're still here.'

In a film of this I would like the part of me to be played by Cary Grant. Don't tell me this is impossible; it's my fantasy. The worker can be played by Sigourney Weaver please, or Tilda Swinton. Okay, so I concede Cary Grant may be unavailable, so someone with my level of baldness but equally devastating good looks, who can make me seem vulnerable but urbane and intelligent.

But.

But you're still here.

Say it with me.

But you're still here.

Amongst the pain of depression, you *can* find a core bit of strength. It's really bloody small – depression hides it; you have to search for it – but I promise you it's there and that's what we need to focus on.

Now, this isn't easy, far from it. It takes practice. I know, I hate that word too. I hate having to practise any-thing, and depression makes it one gazillion times harder. Practice sounds like homework, which makes me think of school and too many associations with being bad at maths; not understanding physics; yucky, sweaty locker rooms; and not being good at football because when I kick the wretched ball it somehow goes off in a completely differ-ent direction to how I intended it and everyone laughs. Bastards.

Right now, I strongly suspect depression is telling you that you're weak and you have no strong bit inside you, that you're different from other people with depression. Yeah, I have that conversation too.

Listen to me: you have strength inside you.

And, hey, you might have depression, but you're not Kim Kardashian's eyebrow-brush cleaner. See, don't you feel better now?

For now, all you need to remember is 'but'. (Stop laughing.)

But you're still here.

But you're still here.

But you're still here.

15. I miss being me – getting over me-phobia.

Depression is about loss.

Once, I tried to count on my fingers all of the things I'd lost due to frigging depression, and then realised I would need to be a mutant with additional digits to do this comprehensively. They included, but are not limited to, the list below.

- My job
- My career
- Some friends
- Joy
- Hope
- Money
- Short-term memory
- Concentration
- Ability to read
- Sleep
- Vitality
- Ability to laugh
- Reasoning ability

But the one I missed most of all was being me.

Depression had taken me over, and the old me was gone. Who was this creature who couldn't sit still? Who was this alien who sat down to read a book only to struggle to get through two sentences? How did I used to do it? Who was this weirdo who turned on the television, watched an advert for two seconds, got angry, turned off the television and flung the remote control out of the window? I missed being the old James, who could do a day's work, come home, cook dinner, then sit and relax. And watch the television.

There was a new normal in town, but the problem was I really hated the new normal me. I had developed 'Me-phobia', which you may not have heard of but I've just made it up, so go with me. It's more than hating yourself: you fear yourself because you're completely unfamiliar with yourself. You don't want to be around yourself because you're a stranger.

Aliens have come down and replaced you with something that looks like you, talks like you but doesn't feel or act like you. It's terrifying. Plus, the aliens are green with yellow spots, which is really scary. And, more importantly, mine hadn't the decency to have given me a full head of hair and a six-pack.

You have to define the new you. The new you that will probably stay around for some time. When I was struggling with who I was, I made a list which looked like this:

- I am more pathetic.
- I am more prone to crying.

- I am more sensitive.
- I am less skilled.
- I am less confident.
- I am less happy.
- I am less able to do anything.
- I am an idiot.

You're not allowed to write a list like this. Okay, I'll be a bit flexible. The rule is you are allowed two of these kinds of negative definitions of yourself if you must but no more. Agreed? Please nod and say, 'Yes, James.' Excellent. Oh, and you're allowed to write this list with someone else if you want, as loved ones can be good at this kind of thing.

Let's do the list again. This is going to be tough, but let's do it.

- I am different to how I was, but that's okay.
- I prioritise myself more.
- I am more aware of my needs.
- I appreciate my own space more.
- I am more tuned in to my body.
- I know more clearly when I need to get help.
- I'm more humble.
- I am less tolerant of rubbish people in my life.

It's a new version of you, like an upgraded computer pro-gramme. Sure, it's under attack from a pretty hefty virus, but it's growing and changing, and the new version is slowly getting better and better.

16. Celebrate small steps (they're actually huge)

I'm in a supermarket, one of those really huge ones that also sells clothes, kitchen equipment, garden furniture and probably personalised cardigans for ferrets if you look hard enough. This is my one trip out a day, to try to get food. The rest of the time I'm too scared to go out. I stay inside, not sleeping, not showering, not living.

I'm going to buy a sandwich. They're usually placed near the entrance so I can be in and out in a few minutes and back hiding in the flat. Sandwiches have certain advantages: I don't need to cook, I don't need to wash a plate, I can eat from the packet on the way home and that will be that.

The entrance to the supermarket is full of plants, picnic tables, barbecues and trays upon trays of wilting plants. Someone is trying get people to donate to a charity which finds missing budgies, and another is handing out tokens for 50p off absinthe mojito popsicles. Or something like that. They are all in my way. I squeeze past the people standing in the entrance on their phones or stopped to examine a dead clematis with their trolley in the way of everyone. I can feel my anger rising and the tears coming.

'Just get the sandwich and get out,' I say to myself. 'Imagine you're in the SAS. The only thing that matters is rescuing the sandwich. There may be casualties, but focus on the sandwich. Just focus on the sandwich.'

I get to where the chilled cabinet of sandwiches usually is and, of course, they've been moved. WHERE ARE THE F***ING SANDWICHES?

I ask a shop assistant.

'WHERE ARE THE F***ING SANDWICHES?'

'Oh, yes . . . Now, let me think. Gosh, I should know this, shouldn't I? Hmm . . . sandwiches, sandwiches, where are they? Oh – I know, aisle nine, dear. No, no . . . wait, wait, that's wrong; aisle nine is feminine hygiene, I think, or cat food – one or the other. So . . . maybe aisle eleven? Yes, why don't you try that.'

'You don't actually know?'

'We just moved it all round this morning, so I'm not too sure. Sorry.'

I walk towards aisle eleven which is, of course, at the far end of the supermarket. I start sweating. People are racing around with their trolleys, not looking where they're going. I speed up, and it seems like they do too. There are a few near misses and then finally someone rams into me. I glare at them as they glare at me, thinking it was my fault. I'm jogging now and somehow hit a small, rat-sized dog. A tartan shopping cart topples over and then a packet of cereal comes dislodged and brings down five other packets.

I get to aisle eleven. I walk up and down twice, but find no sandwiches. This is the New World wine and red-pepper hummus section. I ask another assistant where the sandwiches are.

'Aisle one, by the entrance.'

'I've just been there. Your colleague told me they were here.'

'Well, they were wrong.'

'Obviously.'

'They're next to the crudités and salami. You won't see them from the entrance, but if you head back via the middle aisle, you'll find them.'

I sort of thank him, but it mostly gets lost in a mutter about the stupidity of not being able to see the sandwiches from the entrance.

I walk all the way back to where I started and find the sandwiches. Most have gone as it's 3.30 p.m. What's left is mostly chicken. I don't eat meat. There's an egg and mayonnaise thing that I can smell from inside the packet and a vegetarian kale, smoked carrot, parsnip jus and watermelon melange concoction thing.

'There's more on the other side, dear,' says the assistant I spoke to first.

And there are. Hundreds. All staring at me. I freeze. How the hell did I used to be able to choose things? I could have tuna, or salmon, or cheese, or salad, or flatbread with falafel, or an olive bread baguette. I hate all the sandwiches. I hate this supermarket. I hate all the shop assistants. I hate that ratty dog. I hate the woman that bumped into me, but, most of all, I hate myself. I start to cry and panic. People are looking at me: half of them in fear and the other half in sympathy. But no one comes to check I'm okay. I'm waiting for a Tannoy announcement saying, 'Assistance required. Middle-aged man on aisle one having a breakdown.'

All I blooming need is to pick up one packet of sand-wiches, and it feels like I've been chosen to save the world by sitting a Ph.D. exam in particle physics when I've only got a GSCE grade C in biology. I shut my eyes, grab a packet and head for the self-service tills. I stuff it in my pocket and head home.

It turns out to be that horrible egg mayonnaise thing, which is disgusting. I have sweated all the way through my clothes, I have come out angrier and more anxious than before, but, and this is the really, really, really important point . . .

I GOT THE SANDWICH.

That was ten years ago and by no means at my lowest point, but I'd just done something that most people do every day and don't think about. These things are different with depression. Very different. Small things are huge. Anything that you've managed to achieve, no matter how small you think it is (or how insignificant depression is saying it is), is evidence of your strength. It could be writing a birthday card and posting it, taking out the recycling, paying a bill, buying some winter gloves – it doesn't matter; if it seems small and you achieved it, it counts.

Write these things down. Seriously. Write a note on your phone, on some paper or in macaroni if you want – I don't care – but please record it. You need it to look back on and to give you evidence of the things you *can* do.

Now, go get that sandwich.

17. Get some sleep

'Okay, so if I get five hours' sleep, that will be okay, right? Five hours? That should be enough. But that's if I get to sleep now, which I probably won't. It might take me an hour to get to sleep, so maybe I'll get four hours. I'm going to be tired, but that's just half of what I should be getting, so I'll be weary but I guess okay on four hours. If it's three hours I'm going to struggle, but with three espressos, two cans of energy drink and regular slaps to the face I should be fine. Won't I? Won't I?'

It's 4 a.m. and you're awake.

Again.

Again.

Again.

It's been the same for the past six weeks.

This is brilliant. How excellent to be awake in the darkness with your heart racing. Everyone in the rest of your time zone is asleep, and it's just you gazing at the clock, your mind racing in the darkness. Sleep has become one of those things that other people do. They just go to bed and sleep. Easy, right? Not with depression.

The middle of the night is the worst time for depression. The world is devoid of light and hope. You're all alone. And depression springs to life to let you mull over all the ways you have failed, all the hideous parts of your character and the fact that you will never get better.

Depression loves anything that gives it more power. It loves lack of sleep because it makes all its symptoms one hundred times worse. It will disrupt everything and exacerbate your depression symptoms.

Without sounding too much like a politician, let's get one thing perfectly clear. Sleep is essential to get right when you have depression. Problematic sleeping is one of the first signs of depression starting, and it can continue and get more problematic. You have to tackle it.

The consequences of not getting enough sleep are serious on your physical and mental health. Without enough sleep, I cry even more than I do anyway with depression, I'm dizzy (physically and the forgetful kind too), my memory is rubbish, I can't coordinate and when 3 p.m. comes around my body thinks this is now the perfect time for sleep.

So what do you do?

Going to your doctor and looking at medication to help in the short term is definitely an option. A note of caution:

HOW TO TELL DEPRESSION TO PISS OFF

I got dependent on sleeping pills as I took them for too long. My withdrawals were like fighting a 75-foot dragon with a withering fairy duster, so proceed with caution and get clear medical advice.

There are lots of other options too – again, all in conjunction with medical advice please. There are hypnosis apps, fantastic books, meditation videos and therapists who specialise in getting your circadian rhythms back into place. There's specialist therapy for sleep, and some areas of your country might offer sleep clinics or free treatment plans. All is not lost. It takes effort and energy (tricky when you don't have any because you haven't slept), but try everything to see if it will help.

Then there's all the normal healthy sleep advice too. Not injecting caffeine straight into your blood stream at 11 p.m. at night. Not listening to techno music whilst you're in bed. Not going to the gym at 1 a.m. and then expecting to get a full night's rest afterwards. And not putting on disco lights in the bedroom before you go to sleep. But do put them on in the morning, and dance for all you're worth – which, for the record, is a lot.

18. Read some stories

A few months after being acutely unwell with depression, I really, really wanted to hear from other people who had depression too. I had questions. How did it come about? How did they manage it? What did they do? How were they still living their lives? I needed to read that people could get through this pain and come out the other side.

The first online account I read was from a man who wrote that he met a rainbow-clad angel who told him that he needed to move to Prague to cure his depression. He did as he was told and apparently it worked. Simple. No more depression. I've been to Prague, by the way; it's lovely but it didn't cure my depression. To be fair, I wasn't instructed to go by a rainbow angel, so that might have been the problem. And, for the record, I have nothing against people who see rainbow angels; I'm just jealous that I don't have one who tells me to live in glamorous European capitals.

I found lots of accounts that didn't resonate with me. Ones from people who had developed a special linctus to cure their depression – a secret mixture which included the spleen of a mongoose and a small bag of Arabian cashew nuts. Other people claimed that they had severe depression for a few days, but it disappeared because they simply wished it away.

Then I did a bit more searching and found accounts from people whose depression sounded like mine. They had been through it, suffered from it, but were still here. Maybe it was possible after all?

I read more and more, and watched videos online too. I read that people had the same symptoms that I thought were just peculiar to me. They had the same feeling that depression had turned their life upside down, that they didn't know who they were, who other people were, what anything meant, how the world worked, how to think or how to function properly any more. Their brains had turned into a mush of weirdness, and I nodded because mine had too. People got it. People got the bizarre pain that I thought was just in me. They told me that their memory was awful too, that they wandered around like a zombie maxed out on horse tranquillisers, not knowing what day it was or what a 'day' actually meant. It wasn't just me, and now that I had evidence that others had got through it, were still living with it, then maybe, just maybe, I could too.

We need to hear other people's stories about depression because it validates our own stories and makes us feel less alone. And, crucially, it teaches us things. There's a reason that stories have been handed down and used throughout history. Yes, they entertain, but they're learning aids for how to live.

Spend some time searching for people with stories of your type of depression. The internet was made for this kind of search; there are thousands of blogs out there. If you want to you can (*cough, cough*) look at my website www.therecoveryletters.com or buy *The Recovery Letters* book (*cough*). It's up to you, but if you buy my other book, you will help my cat not to starve, so you know, it's your choice.

When I was searching, I found Rose's story. She wrote that depression had contributed to her marriage breaking up and had lost all hope. Then I discovered an account from Simon, who had to spend time in psychiatric hospital and with crisis services. I read their stories and saw that I'm just like them; depression had done awful things to them too. I read how Rose gets through her day with help from her sister and how Simon is supported with anti-depressants, and I thought maybe I could learn something from them. Now, Rose is in a new relationship – it's early days but she's happy, and she's with someone who understands her illness. Simon is working again in a job that he can manage and cares about. I think, 'Good for them.' I loved reading that depression hadn't kept them down.

I can learn from them because I am one of them. We all are.

19. Depression? You're having a laugh, aren't you?

It's 3 p.m. I'm sat watching television – a sitcom, one of my favourites I've seen countless times. I know every line and upcoming joke. I know the storyline and the set, and I know what will happen at the end of the programme. I'm also recovering from a suicide attempt the night before. (I write this just to lighten the mood a little – all this depression business can get you down.)

The night before, I took lots of sleeping pills, washed down with a very cheap and crude Spanish red wine. Why I didn't opt for the much nicer Italian bottle on the top of the kitchen cabinets – especially considering I thought it was going to be my last drop – I have no idea. I guess you don't really think clearly when you're trying to calculate how many pills will stop you breathing.

Spoiler alert: I didn't die! Hooray! I woke up twenty hours later with a very sore head (damn that cheap Spanish plonk), still very sleepy, depression still whirring around my head and cursing my inability to do maths, which probably kept me alive.

So I'm sat on the sofa, watching a sitcom. All the characters are reassuringly still there, suspended in time. The laughter track repeats and life plays out as it always had. The first few jokes come and go, and I don't laugh as I normally would have. But I do smile. I smile at the ridiculousness of the scene, at the character failing to get what she wants, at the absurdity of it all. I smile because I know exactly what is going to happen in the next thirty-minute episode; that everything in this fictional world is going to be all right. My smiles are small but they're there.

In the midst of my gnawing pain, suicidal thoughts and the dark sludge that is my life, there is still laughter. It's coming from fictional characters in borrowed clothes on a set in a television studio probably in the middle of an industrial estate, but it reminds me that I used to laugh, and that other people still laugh. It tells me that not everything in the world is how I currently see it. I can suspend disbelief for a while and lose myself in this sitcom world of nonsense. A world where people fall out and get back together with ease, where there is always a quirky friend next door and a part-human pet. And if there is laughter out there, then maybe one day I will laugh as I used to.

These days, I use comedy and humour when I'm feeling good so I can hear and feel myself laughing and know that it's still possible. But I use it mostly when I'm in pain because it reveals another world where there is silliness and mirth. It's a world far away from where I am, but I have to counteract depression, stand up to the bully that it is. Sometimes, the smiles are so small I can barely feel them inside me, but I'm fighting back. And even if there is only a slight change, a small, split-second change in my mood when I hear a joke or someone falls over, then it's worth it.

Aim for small smiles when the laughter won't come.

20. Second by second – not day by day

I'm at the beach, which is two minutes away from home. I've run out of the flat and I'm sitting on the pebbles, staring at the sea, hoping that it will come and swallow me up or maybe a seagull will drop something magical into my brain and soothe out all the emotional pain.

Neither happens.

'I can't do this. I can't manage the pain,' I say out loud.

The wind swallows most of my words, which is probably a good thing as I don't want to frighten the old woman who is cleaning up her dog's poo a few metres away.

If this were a novel, a kind stranger (maybe the woman with the dog) would come and sit by me, talk to me, comfort me and give me strength to carry on. Or I would observe a crab struggling up the wet sea wall and be inspired to keep going and climb my own metaphorical wall. Or maybe a mermaid would swim to the shoreline, invite me for a swim and I'd be magically be turned into one of them. I'm fairly sure merpeople don't have depression, so I'd go and live with them.

But, of course, there is no stranger, the woman with the dog has disappeared (possibly due to my shouting), I've never seen a crab on this beach and, as much as I wait, no mythical sea people appear. Bastards. I take this as a personal slight. If they knock on my door wanting some wax for their scales, I'll shut the door in their face. If they wash up on the beach and need pushing back in, I'll haughtily turn my head and ignore their agonising screams.

I could do any number of sensible things. I could go back home and talk to my husband, I could phone a friend, I could phone a helpline, I could call my mental health crisis service, I could go for a cycle, I could throw some stones in the sea. But I can't, I'm paralysed with the pain and the whole entire bastard marine community have disowned me.

How am I going to get to work tomorrow if I feel like this? How am I going to meet my friend for coffee the following day? How will I get on a train in the middle of the week and go to the birthday party that I've promised to attend? How am I going to take a bath or get to sleep?

I do nothing. I sit and look at my watch and see the seconds pass.

Then, without the help of a crab, or stranger or mermaid, I realise that I've got through and survived each second that has passed. I keep looking at my watch. More seconds pass and I'm still here. I'm still here. Shit, I'm still here.

Taking things day by day is pointless when you're in this kind of pain. A day is forever. A day is a year, a decade, a lifetime, an endless sprawl of fear in front of you.

So don't think in days, don't think in hours or moments: think in seconds.

Watch the seconds pass and notice how you get through each one. Once you've got through one second, you can get through the next and the next and the next. And the next.

I keep looking at my watch and the seconds slow down my brain. I don't rush into the sea with heavy stones in my pants. I don't try to hit my head on the sea wall. I keep looking at my watch for a few minutes, counting the seconds, and then I stand up and walk home.

It took around one hundred seconds to read this chapter, and you're still here too. That's amazing. Now on to the next chapter.

21. Do the work when you're well

A short play about painting a bedroom.

SEAN: I've done my back in.

HELEN: Oh, I'm sorry to hear that.

SEAN: But I'm going to paint the bedroom.

HELEN: You're going to paint the bedroom with a bad back?

SEAN: Yeah, I think it will work out okay.

HELEN: Do you really think that's a good idea?

SEAN: Yeah, should be fine.

HELEN: But, won't you hurt your back more and do a bad paint job?

SEAN: Ummm . . . I don't think so.

HELEN: Can you move?

SEAN: I can't move at all. I'm in bed. I can't wash, get to the toilet, cook food or go to work.

HELEN: And how high is the ceiling?

SEAN: About 20 feet.

Silence.

HELEN: Hey, I've got a superb idea! Don't paint the bedroom now, paint the bedroom when your back is better.

SEAN: Oh, do you think so?

HELEN: Yeah, it just came to me! If you paint the bedroom when you're better, you won't hurt your back and you'll do an awesome paint job.

SEAN: You're a genius.

And . . . scene.

The time to work on recovery from depression (or paint the bedroom walls) is when you're well. When you're unwell, you need all your energy to get through the day.

When I'm unwell, I often make extreme decisions. Or at least think about them. 'Yes!' I think, 'I know! The solution to all my problems is to move to Bhutan and open a hamster café,' or I'll give up my job, retrain as a zoo keeper and specialise in the mating rituals of South American white capybaras. Sometimes I buy ridiculous things on the internet, which is why I ended up with a giant outdoor paint-gun thing that never worked and 150 red geraniums. I wish I was exaggerating.

When you're feeling better, your mind is in a much clearer state to reflect on what you need. I make better decisions that are more reasoned and not infected with depression's voice. This is the time to sign up to the park run, to contact friends and arrange to meet up, to read more about depression and to engage with others. When you're well, you should do all the work that is impossible to do when you're ill.

This is also the time to write down what you want to happen when you're ill. Make a plan for yourself and share it with your close loved ones, who may need to intervene when you're unwell.

My plan simply involves a scale of 1 to 10, and I call it the shittiness scale. I've copyrighted this, so no stealing it, okay? All right, I'll let you use it, but no one else. I use it to gauge how ill I feel, and at what point I need to get some help. At 1–3, I'm fine; 4–5 is okayish – I can manage. At 6, I need to actively do things to improve my mood; 7 means I might need a day off work or some time asleep; 8 means I'm pretty ill and need help from a support service; 9 means I'm feeling suicidal; and at 10 I am actively making plans to take my life. It's a bit of a crude and brutal system, but it works for me. I have a copy of it and if I'm unable to help myself, I can usually get someone else involved to call services for me, because at 8 I tend to think I'm not worthy of any help and that nothing will help.

Remember, listen to Helen; she knows what she's talking about.

22. Intrude on the intrusive thoughts

It's morning and I'm heading to work. I leave my flat and start walking to the train station.

'You're a bloody pillock, you're a pillock, you're a pillock. You're a pillock, you're a pillock, you're a pillock.'

Depression is shouting at me, screaming obscenities and it's filling my head.

I cross the road at the traffic lights and it's still shouting.

'You're a fat, ugly, hideous excuse for a human being.'

I walk past the church and go up the hill.

'You're a stupid, worthless, failure with smelly feet.'

Then, to add to this sublime experience, an image of a gun pressed against my temples appears.

The gun goes off, explodes and my brains fly all over the place, narrowly missing a passing Alsatian puppy and a recycling bin.

The gun is smoking and my brain has gone, which is somewhat inconvenient.

Despite not having a functioning head, I continue towards the train station.

'You're a disgusting, worthless, unlovable idiot who doesn't deserve to live.'

I finally reach the station and there are way too many people – real people – blocking my way.

'I could kick that person in front, I hate them so much. I would smear them with that dog poo. But, actually, you're more like that dog poo, you rancid, useless pile of crap.'

I get to the platform, manage to sit down on a bench and gently rock myself.

'Row, row, row your boat gently down the ... pathetic fuck up that is your life.'

The train is, of course, running late.

'I can't do this. I hate myself. I can't do this.'

It's been five minutes since I left my house, and this has been the running commentary of intrusive thoughts and images in my head that I have no control over. It's like a television has been implanted in my brain, randomly switching channels. But it's one of those really terrible channels that are way down the list, the kind you only go to when there is nothing else on. Past all the dreadful shopping channels selling battery-powered ice skates and self-assembly lawn mowers, but before the deluge of adult channels. It's like I've got the remote control in my hands and I'm desperately pressing all the buttons, trying to curb the chaos, but nothing works.

'Stop, stop, stop, STOP,' I say in my head. I don't say this out loud, as I will scare myself and the nice pigeon on the station desperately hoping for some crumbs.

The thoughts and images pause for a few seconds.

'You're a filthy gobshite, full of . . .'

'STOP, STOP, STOP!'

Some silence, and then it's back again.

'If you're happy and you know it, kill yourself!'

'STOP, STOP, F***ING STOP.'

The thing about intrusive thoughts is that they are bloody rude. Who comes into your head uninvited, that's what I want to know? So we have to go on the attack again; we intrude on the intrusive thoughts – give 'em a taste of their own medicine. Start talking back and interrupting them; see how they like it.

'You ain't the boss of me,' I say in my head. You can do this in any accent you choose but I opt for a kind of East End London gangster-ish sort of voice. 'Go on, do one. Piss off with yer. Did you 'ear me?'

You have to shout louder, be stronger and keep shouting until the intrusive thoughts start to back down.

'You think you're the boss of me? Do yer? You are nothing. Nothing, I tell you. You are dead to me, you despicable low life.'

The thoughts may well start to come back, but this is war; keep on shouting.

'You are a speck of dust on the anus of the time. You are a sodden, shite-filled, boil of pus, and I'm gonna burst ya.'

I realise that this is shouting at your own mind but, trust me, you have to. The feeling of 'otherness' and invasion with depression is really strong, so it's not actually that weird.

In terms of tactics, or war planning, you can opt for retreat if you want. You can put some music on with headphones or watch films. But the aim is to prove to the thoughts you aren't going to back down when they come back next time, so I think an all-out assault is the better way to go.

Some people will tell you that 'a thought is just a thought' and that thoughts can't hurt you because they're not actions, so you shouldn't worry too much about it. 'Let the thoughts slip away across your mind like a cloud in the sky,' they say. When my depression is bad, my thoughts are powerful, painful and damaging, and they need to be spoken back to. If I try to get my thoughts to slip away like a cloud, they reverse, point machine guns at me and try to kill me. Lovely, eh?

Do all the things that a Victorian parent would tell their child not to. Be a street urchin in a Dickens novel. Talk back, be rude, interrupt, swear, challenge, don't back down and generally be a nuisance to depression.

23. Be, like, totally nice to others

Buy scented summer flowers representing peace and love for other people. Bless those around you with your gratitude and your everlasting adoration. Sprinkle their aura with stars of togetherness and vow everlasting commitment. Help small children on the path to righteousness. Cherish the wisdom of the elderly, and revere them as the sages they are. Above all, emit the wafts of compassion wherever you go and smile continuously until your cheek muscles crack.

Now cross out the above paragraph. This is not what I mean by being nice to others – although if you want to sprinkle my aura, go right ahead. The fact is that doing small, achievable, practical favours for other people helps your depression.

Be warned though that when you're unwell with depression you can't get too caught up in other people's issues. So don't go and volunteer for a crisis helpline or

decide you're going to be a counsellor or the head of the
United Nations. What I mean is when you're in a shop, help
the person get down a can of beans that they can't reach.
Give your seat up on the train to somebody who needs it.
Offer to do some weeding for the person next door if they
can't bend down too well any more. Wave to the children
from the train. Say thank you to the person who let you
pass when you were running for the bus. Feed the ducks.

Practical, small, achievable acts are the key here. If
you've offered to paint the garden walls for the whole
street, that's way too much. If you've decided to take in
every stray cat across a 30-mile radius, that's going to
make for a very smelly house. If you've volunteered to fly to
Mongolia at your own expense to mentor distressed camel
herders in their native Mongolian, you're going to be . . .
well, I'm not sure, but it's a really bad idea.

It's not always going to work out smoothly, so be pre-
pared for some bumps. Once I helped a man with three
screaming young children in tow when his shopping had
fallen out of his basket. He thanked me and then said,
'Glad it was you helped me and not those bloody scroung-
ing immigrants. They only think of their own. Can't
stand them.' Then I felt bad for helping this racist pig and
wanted to tip all his shopping on the floor again.

But when it works out it's wonderful – like receiving
a small electric charge of hope. It's a glimpse away from

depression into a window showing that niceness exists. You realise that you can be nice, that other people can be nice and the world, sometimes, is a great place – even if you only feel it for a few seconds.

Seeing that you can still be useful makes you realise feel that depression is not all of you. A tangible, manage-able act proves you're still worthy, you're still able to help, even though you're struggling to help yourself.

24. Get your identity tags

I can see a man in the pew two rows in front of me. He looks grey, his eyes are staring and black, he is gazing ahead at no fixed point, but I feel like he's looking for something. He hasn't shaved. It isn't a cultivated stubble; he just looks a mess. His coat has white dog hairs on the back.

'He's a depressive,' says my mum, kindly, seeing me look at him.

'Oh,' I say. 'He looks sad . . . Can I have a dog?'

'No, you can't, you have a Russian hamster called Dusty,' says my mum.

And that was the end of the conversation about the depressed man.

Growing up, there weren't any words for the feelings I had. Things have changed a lot, which is brilliant. Now we can see celebrities talking about their own depression. People do TV shows and podcasts and books just about this one illness. When I grew up this didn't exist.

I am not depression. I am definitely, definitely (definitely) not a 'depressive'. I am James, who has a cat that goes for walks and has a wonderful husband, and too many red geraniums, and friends who like gin too. I'm an indulgent uncle and a son, a brother, a brother-in-law and a tennis nerd. I watch too many Real Housewives programmes, I read cosy crime novels and I have depression.

Depression is not all of my identity, but it's definitely a part of me which I don't hide because having a diagnosis helps me makes sense of the feelings I have. It validates that the weird thoughts, senses and moods that I thought were only peculiar to me are part of a greater illness, something experienced by many, many people. Knowing that I have depression and using that term to describe my illness allows me to reach out, research and remember that it's not just me.

I also know that, at times, our identity tags can hang heavy around our necks. This is mostly an invisible illness, but when people know we have depression they love to judge and make assumptions. Admittedly, we all make judgements. At the moment I'm judging your trouser and cardigan combination – and it's not good. See? But the judgements about depression can sting and stigmatise.

'It's just that, well, you never *seem* like you have depression,' said a friend. 'You're always, so . . . I don't know, so happy.'

'I really don't get it,' said a colleague. 'How can you feel so bad that you want to take your own life?'

I take a few deep breaths. Unfortunately, I'm not allowed to garrotte people – it's illegal or something – so I try to explain about depression. Sometimes they get it, sometimes they get some of it but still look perplexed, and sometimes, after a long conversation, they still shake their heads, utterly clueless. Then I garrotte them.

Like any process of 'coming out', and I've done this a fair few times in my life, there is danger and hurt, but ultimately it frees you. It's not that I'm proud of my depression – it's too awful to feel pride – but I am determined not to bow to the shame that some people, and the illness itself, want me to feel.

Once you start talking about having depression, you find that other people have permission to talk about their own mental health too. Then they tell you that their brother has depression, and their aunt and their friend do too, and they're pretty sure their giant African land snail is exhibiting symptoms of dysthymia. Then you feel less alone; you feel it's not just you, and the circle of understanding widens.

Hiding your depression feeds the fuel of shame, and as we know, depression LOVES shame, because then it can blame everything on you. So let's all say:

'I have depression. It's something I live with. It's come about because of experiences I've had and how my body works. I hate it, but I live alongside it.'

No, I'm not proud of the illness I have, but I'm proud of how I manage it. I fight not to feel ashamed, and without sounding too much like your secondary-school head teacher at the end-of-term prize-giving, I'm really proud of you too.

25. There are many other crazies out there

Imagine you're walking along the street, off to post a letter and then nose around the charity shops for some new cushions. You stop in a coffee shop, sit outside with your latte and watch the people go by. Now, I want you to count every seventh person. One, two, three, four, five, six, seven. Imagine that every seventh person has depression like you. Every single one of them suffers as you do. Look at the older man with the jaunty suit, the mother with two small children, the middle-aged guy with a sausage dog in tow, the teenager with headphones, the lady with the flowery dress blowing in the wind, the person with sunglasses, the twenty-something checking their phone. Look at them as they pass by. They're like you. They're one of you.

Now it's 2 a.m. and you're still awake. It's pitch black outside and depression is thumping you in the head with a hammer. Anxiety (depression's, like, total bestie) is hitting you on the head with a hammer too, just for symmetry.

You get up and look out of the window. There's the vague orange glare of a street lamp over the road. You're sweating.

When people tell me 'You're not alone,' I often feel furious. How is that supposed to help me exactly? Are you all going to come and make me feel better? Are you all going to club together to fundraise for a special syringe to drain the depression out of my mind? What's going to happen?

There are 300 million people all over the world who suffer from depression. That's ... well, it's a heck of a lot of people. Let's say there might be 100,000 million people also awake or feeling rubbish at the same time as you. If you count those people, then you'll probably get to sleep, but what I want you to do when you're still awake at 2 a.m. is imagine them.

Imagine these people in great detail. Imagine their faces, the shape of their noses, their hair, what their names are, what jobs they have, if they have families, their favourite colours, their hobbies – as much as you can fit into your mind's eye as possible. Are they repulsed by broccoli? Maybe they're terrified of bees. Imagine them all.

Then think about all those feelings that depression gives you, which are deep inside of you. Those that you think you're the only one experiencing. Then imagine all those people with the same feelings too – all over the world, millions of people, also feeling alone, looking out into the darkness and thinking of you.

We feel alone. Depression tells us we are alone. We're not; we're united by these feelings.

26. Cut down on the booze

I have something to tell you. Please don't hate me. You're not going to like this. It's me, not you. I don't mean to hurt you. Honestly, if there was another way, I would tell you.

Let's say this really quickly so it won't be too painful:

Drinking alcohol makes your depression worse.

Now, I wouldn't blame anyone who tried to self-medicate with alcohol to take away the nasty thoughts of depression for a while and to fall into oblivion. I've done it myself. I've wanted so badly to escape from the pain that alcohol was one way of doing it. The issue is that alcohol is a depressant drug. If you mix a depressant with your depression, you don't need to be Antoine Lavoisier to work out that it's not going to be good. No, I didn't know who Antoine Lavoisier was either, but he's 'the father of modern chemistry' so I reckon he would have known about this. Mind you, he lived in eighteenth-century France, probably eating flambé squirrel with Roquefort cheese every day, and had his head cut off in the French Revolution, so who's laughing now, Antoine? Eh?

You don't need to give up alcohol altogether, and the good news is that as you get older a hangover lasts three days and you feel like hell has opened its gates to unleash all its powers into your head and stomach anyway. I still have a drink. There's nothing quite like the sound of ice cubes gently cracking into a cold gin as the tonic hits them, the fizz mixing beautifully and the delicate juniper flavour reaching out and tantalising you . . . silently you start screaming 'More, more! Give me another taste, you dark temptress!'

107

Where was I? Yes, so I still have a drink from time to time but with the full knowledge that if I drink too much my depression is going to be horrific the next day. After the first six hundred times, you come to realise that this illness is hard enough to live with without something that can expand and exaggerate it by 300 per cent, in three easy pint glasses.

I'm okay with one drink, although it will disrupt my sleep. Two drinks and the next day I can feel my mood is definitely lower. Three drinks and depression will wake me in the middle of the night, and it goes downhill from there. Four drinks in I'm wanting to voluntarily head to the guillotine with our mate Antoine.

Sometimes it's worth it. You want a drink at a wedding, or you're out with friends you haven't seen for ages, or you've been studying eighteenth-century French chemists for hours and need a break. Then the trick is, when depression comes a-calling the next day, see it for what it is and tell yourself it's worse because of the alcohol. Awareness helps us to challenge the status quo.

Now, you might be all like, 'James, how can alcohol be a depressant when it makes me giggle and dance like a demented elf, and I tell everyone I see, including the taxi driver on the way home, that I love them?' Well, it's because alcohol excites you and lowers your inhibitions, but it's going to whack you the next day when it's leaving your system.

The other problem is anxiety. My nightmare scenario is being at a party with hundreds of extroverts who I don't know. I have to go alone. Everyone seems younger, funnier, better looking, better dressed and richer than me. It's at a swanky London club where it's too cool to have a front door or a street number and you have to knock in a secret sequence to gain entrance. You are then met by a sulky coat person who looks at you like you've just thrown up on their Gucci fur slippers, and you have to give them a tip for the privilege of being on the receiving end of their attitude. Everyone is talking to everyone else, the host is no where to be seen and the music is like something Beelzebub has composed whilst he was enduring a particularly bad bout of food poisoning. I need a drink.

But remember: alcohol doesn't help anxiety in the long run. It doesn't give you confidence; it just makes you care less. In the scenario above, that's no doubt a good thing, but be aware of its ability to increase your anxiety the next day, which is a nasty accompaniment to depression.

Understand what alcohol does and doesn't do. Remember the effect it can have, and proceed with caution.

Righty ho, so who's up for a soft drink then?

27. Get a hobby – get a toolbox

I'm rubbish at fixing things. I mean, really bad. Seriously, don't hand me your broken vase or faulty laptop as they'll come back looking a hundred times worse. And this isn't self-deprecation: it's just the sad truth.

I do love toolboxes though – rummaging through the discarded nails, brushing past metal implements that all look like sausage makers, with the sweet hope that some-where in the bottom will be something new and delicious and extraordinary. With depression, you need a toolbox of coping mechanisms at hand to help. Not a real toolbox obviously; a set of steel pliers isn't going to help your depression.

A range of hobbies can distract us from the pain. Activity helps us process the experience of depression and lets us engage in something much more meaningful than our illness. Because depression takes away our existing coping mechanisms just when we need them, we have to try new things. Suppressing depression's voice with an activity doesn't take it away, but it masks it for a while to give us a break. Doing is resting for the chattering poison of depression in our minds.

There are *so* many things we can't do with depression that it's hard to find something that works. Our concentration is so affected that it's not easy to start something, and when you do it's easy to give up. The trick is to have a really good rummage through a toolbox of hobbies and interests and to try lots of them. If something doesn't work after you've had a decent try, go for something else and try not to feel that sense of failure; it's just something that isn't right for you.

I've tried a whole heap of stuff over the years. I wrote some truly awful stories, which were full of teenage angst (in my forties) and too many split infinitives (no, I don't know what they are either). I volunteered on an allotment and was superb at digging up weeds but atrociously bad at planting seeds – and everything else vaguely horticultural. Apparently, you can't just pour hundreds of seeds into a small hole and expect large healthy carrots to appear – who knew? I tried to knit. That went really well; let's just say the cat has had fun tearing my 'scarf' into pieces.

There are things that work really well for me though. I cycle a lot. When I was acutely ill, I cycled up and down the coast where I live every day. I cycled up hills, cursing, and down hills, with relief. I couldn't go to the gym, as the feeling of getting nowhere was heightened, so at least when I was cycling it felt like I was moving forward.

For years I couldn't read any books, which was previously my number one means of escape. Slowly, as I got better, I was able to read more. I've never got back to the amount that I was reading before I was ill, but I still read, and every time I turn a page it feels like I'm doing something for me – something that takes me away from my illness.

That sense of achievement is really important, however small. It could be doing a line of crochet, hiking to the top of a hill (however little), taking a photo you're pleased with, baking a quiche that looks at least a little like the picture in the cookbook, painting a picture. It's all proof that you're living and doing something constructive, despite all the things you can't do. Hobbies will make your brain useful again. They will prove to you that your mind is not broken, that you are capable and depression hasn't beaten you.

When you are able to do a hobby or activity, do it with all your might, because the mental health mugger, depression, might come and take it from you for a while. So when I can read books, I try to get through as many pages as I can, and I put two fingers up to depression as I do it. When I can cycle, I go for long ones along the sea and each pedal I turn I grin and swear at depression.

Expressing your depression creatively can be really helpful too. One day, after attending a pottery session for people with depression, I came back home with a bowl the shape of a squashed savoy cabbage. 'I'm just not sure . . . well, I don't really think – I mean, it's lovely, obviously, but I'm not sure pottery is your thing, sweetie,' said my husband, tilting his head and examining the bowl thoroughly. But I had an amazing time pummelling that bowl and pretending it was depression, and who cares that you can't actually put anything into it. And those terrible stories I used to write made me feel better. I was getting stuff out, putting words on a page, and it all helped. I am never going to be Henry Moore or Charles Dickens, but the process of creating is just as important as the sense of achievement. By the way my 'bowl' is still for sale on eBay; it's been on there for six years now. For God's sake, someone make me an offer.

Why not give horse riding a go? Or try sewing felt handbags, or making a toy armadillo, or running around the local park, or caring for carnivorous indoor plants, or life drawing (taking part counts too), or building sandcastles, or writing poetry, or playing croquet, or line dancing, or making stained-glass windows, or baking bread rolls in the shape of The Beatles, or simply going for a walk.

Oh, and if all else fails, buy a cat – they're awesome.

28. It's okay if depression sometimes wins*

I know we're trying to get depression to piss off and every-thing, but listen: if you have a day when depression takes you over, it's okay. I have many of those days.

Sometimes, it all gets too much and I head for bed. I get my headphones, I get some very sugary cereal, I get a blan-ket, I get my cat (whether he likes it or not), I get a squishy cushion and I get my phone. I shut the curtains, turn off the light and hunker down. If I'm going to let depression do its thing, then I'm going to get as comfortable as I can.

If I can cry, then I really weep. I let every wave of self-loathing plummet into me. I feel all the fear and paranoia. I hear depression telling me that things won't get better. I let all of my body feel the excruciating pain. I

---

* It doesn't really win.

go into a foetal position and let it all in. The cat freaks out at this point and jumps off the bed, but I hug the blanket tighter. I breathe out and say, 'Okay, you got me. For now, you win, depression; you have me in your grip, but only for now.'

It's a bit like the South American ayahuasca ceremony (google it), where you have to take the poison to get out the other side. You have to experience a slice of hell to exorcise some of the pain and get to a better place.

Feeling the full pain of depression on occasions, and not fighting it for a while, gives you strength afterwards. It's the same feeling when you cry. You feel awful, the pain is horrendous, but then afterwards something has been released and you feel better.

29. This is your early warning call

Beep, beep, beep! (That's me making the sound of an alarm clock.)

Depression sometimes gives you warning signs that it's on its way. It's like a slow, stinky fart that you can start to sniff a few days beforehand. Sorry, but that's the only way I can think about it. You have to practise sniffing every day to see if you can smell anything. Some people call this mindfulness; I call this 'smelling depression', which admittedly is not such an appealing or commercial concept. You don't get 'smelling depression' colouring books.

Now, there are times when depression gives you no warning at all – you're sat on the train and a guff explodes on the top of your head and there's nothing you can do about it. All you can do is smell the fumes and get out of there as soon as you can. I often get guffed, but I usually get fart warnings too. Again, sorry about the metaphors.

To try to smell depression you have to spend a few minutes checking in every day. Does something feel a little off? Are you more tired than usual, are there aches in your bones, are you teary or is your mood constantly changing? Is your sleep weird, is your appetite weird, do you feel weird, *are* you weird? All these could be signs of depression looming – the stirring of a scent brewing within you.

If you suspect depression is on its way, you can try to do something about it. Get a gas mask or start to treat yourself differently.

For me, I can detect depression when I do too much. If I'm rushing around, having committed to too many things, sleep will be impossible, my concentration will disappear and my appetite goes from not eating anything during the day to gobbling tinned peaches in the middle of the night. It's always tinned peaches – I don't know why.

Then I know that I have to change things. I cancel plans – which I really, really hate doing because then depression tells me I am a useless friend, colleague, brother, uncle, brother-in-law, son, husband, etc. I have to take time to conserve energy and have a few days of sitting watching television.

Admittedly, if you have thirteen children, a goat and two passive-aggressive gerbils, taking time out like this would be hard, but reducing your load is the point here. If I can manage the shame and guilt, then I can often keep a depression episode at bay, or at least lessen the sharpness of it.

Stress is the other big smell. It is the daddy of all farts that can cause depression to appear within a short space of time, or the smell can drift over after many years. No amount of stress is worth a more broken you. Having depression is bad enough without increasing the frequency of the episodes or making the pain significantly worse. Accepting that well-paid promotion isn't worth it if you have to work twice as much, get home late, eat badly, worry all weekend about the week to come and then eventually your depression worsens. Becoming chair of the annual charity frog-racing event isn't worth it if you also have to run the sheep-racing event, the rubber-duck racing event and have agreed to foster three vicious Vietnamese pot-bellied pigs.

Nothing is worth making depression worse – nothing. Not more money, not more prestige, not more animal racing, not the satisfaction of being a pig fosterer.

Look out for the signs; smell them coming before they overtake you.

30. Ditch your crap friends

There will, inevitably, be people in your life that don't really 'get' depression.

They can't understand why you aren't the lovable, happy, bouncy creature you once were. They might start to text less or when you meet up ask, 'You're better now then, are you?' which leaves little room for replying, 'Well, actually my psychiatrist has increased my medication, I spent all of yesterday in bed, I haven't had a shower since last Wednesday and if you're wondering what that smell is, it's because my pants are being continually turned inside out as I haven't the energy to use the washing machine.'

We change with depression; it's unavoidable.

Here's a conversation I had with a friend:

FRIEND: I'm just really worried about you.

ME: I'm worried about me too.

FRIEND: I just want you to be better.

ME: So do I.

FRIEND: You're just really different. You're not the person I used to know.

ME: I miss me as well.

FRIEND: I don't know what to do.

ME: Me neither.

A more useful conversation would be:

ME: I hate this.

FRIEND: Depression sucks. Let's do this together. Remember, I love you.

Some people I know have opted out of my life because they couldn't manage the new ill me. It took me a long time to realise this wasn't my fault. 'Maybe if I try to be a bit brighter when I see them,' I would think. 'Or I could try to not talk about depression, that will make things less awkward for them.' 'If I try to hold it together and not cry, this will make it easier.' Never mind ignoring the elephant in the room, this was like ignoring the man repeatedly hitting me on the head with a baseball bat, and both of us pretending that he didn't exist, he didn't have a baseball bat and wasn't hitting me.

This will sound harsh, but you don't need baseball-bat

deniers in your life. In fact, they could be much more damaging than the baseball bat because they won't let you talk about the big thing in your life, which is depression, and you need to talk about it.

As well as people who have opted out, I have made the choice to opt people out too. It's a difficult decision, but friendships and relationships take energy and commitment from both sides. One friend avoided talking to me about my depression, as if it was contagious if we spoke about it together. They would talk about themselves: what they did last week, what films they'd seen, how their job was going, what they were having for tea, what the royal family were up to, how to make home-made soya bean curd – anything at all rather than talk about how I was. And just when there was a pause in the conversation and I thought, 'Oh, maybe they'll ask about how I am now,' they filled the gap with comments about how they'd seen a chicken the size of a horse on the internet or how to stop mildew in the bathroom with apple cider vinegar and a slice of pickled courgette.

After a while I realised it wasn't going to work. I started to understand that if they couldn't be with me where I was now, then we were going to have to take a break, maybe a permanent one. So slowly I started to see less of them. We didn't have a huge argument in the park; I didn't send them a vicious text message about their crapness as a friend – I didn't have the energy for that. They couldn't handle it, I couldn't handle them not handling it, so I let it fade. They opted out and so did I. It was for the best. Maybe we will reconnect later in life – I don't know – but for now I don't need them around.

Take an inventory of the people in your life and how they've reacted to you having depression. Is there anyone who makes comments like, 'I just don't see why you need to take medication for it,' or 'Yeah, I get depression too, every Monday morning.'? These people need a large warning label stuck on them: 'Danger! Do not approach. Toxic and unhelpful.'

Non-supportive people will sap you of the tiny amounts of energy that you need to manage depression. I got tired of having to explain to people about what depression was and wasn't. 'No, it's not just being sad.' 'No, I can't just snap out of it.' 'No, it's not like the time you were upset when you saw your cat eat a shrew.' 'No, the pills don't make me ecstatically happy.' 'No, it's not because I'm weak'. 'No, it isn't exactly like the time [*insert a celebrity of your choice*] went to rehab for 'stress' after their Malibu lemon tree got an incurable disease.' Seriously, if you don't understand depression then there's a thing called the internet you can use to find out about it. Don't view my illness differently just because of what you've heard or what your own judgements lead you to think.

Good, solid friends and relatives who are supportive, flexible, non-judgemental and loving are the best people to have around you, and they are worth cherishing. If you can get a solid cheerleading squad of these types behind you, then that will work even better. Of course, an actual cheerleading squad behind you would ultimately become irritating and rather scary: all that relentless positivity and pom-poms – bloody hell. But imagine all those people in your life who are rooting for you as your team. They're not always physically with you, but they're thinking of you and wanting the best for you.

31. Yeah, cheers, thanks a lot

I'm a polite kind of person. I believe in please and thank
you and being grateful for being bought a pint by your best
mate. But with depression it's hard to feel grateful for
anything, especially depression itself.

125

When it was first suggested to me that I start to make a
list of things I was grateful for, I spat out my coffee. Not a
great reaction, but thankfully there were paper towels on
hand to mop up my friend Emma's T-shirt.

> ME: What? You want me to be grateful for the intrusive
> thoughts and the pain and the suicidal ideation and the
> lack of motivation and the lack of concentration and the
> self-harm and the memory loss and . . .
>
> EMMA: I know, I know, but listen: that's exactly why you
> should do it.

I had a think. Damn, she had a point. I hate it when that
happens.

I bought a special notebook – my 'Gratitude journal' I was supposed to call it, but I named it 'Stuff that I'm sort of thankful for', which sounded better to me and less like I had to remember to thank the special dew on the grass each day. I sat down with my notebook and pen in hand and thought . . . Nothing came to mind. Was I supposed to be grateful for the gift of laughter or the ability to feel compassion for a dying woodlouse? Was I supposed to be thankful for my nice jacket that I just got from a second-hand shop or the fact that it hadn't rained today? How was I supposed to do this? I phoned Emma.

> ME: You know this whole gratitude business thingy that I'm supposed to be doing?
>
> EMMA: Yep.
>
> ME: Well, how does it work again? Am I supposed to be thankful for each of the sun's rays, for all the sea-weed on the beaches, for the gravel on my driveway and the dwarf planet Pluto? Because if I am, I really don't see the point.
>
> EMMA: You're supposed to look at your regular life and see what you're grateful for having in it.
>
> ME: So I don't need to thank the dwarf planet Pluto?
>
> EMMA: Is it a major part of your everyday life?
>
> ME: Well, no.

EMMA: Then don't include it. And, seriously, what's with you and Pluto?

ME: I just feel sorry for it being downgraded from a proper planet.

EMMA: For goodness sake.

ME: So, what, I'm supposed to be grateful for breakfast cereal and decaf coffee?

EMMA: James, are you being deliberately stupid? Listen, who's in your life at the moment?

ME: Husband, cat, friends, family, work colleagues, I guess.

EMMA: And are you grateful for having them in your life?

ME: Yes, well, some of them.

EMMA: Then those are the people to write down and include. It might change each day, but that's okay, and it's okay if it stays the same. What else helps your day?

ME: I like it when I can read my book.

EMMA: Good, write that down.

ME: I like it when I can go cycling.

EMMA: Great, write that down too.

ME: Okay, I think I understand it a bit more.

EMMA: Brilliant. (*Silence.*) James?

ME: Yep.

EMMA: You can write down Pluto if you want.

ME: Oh, thank goodness.

I try to write something every day. Some days I write lots of things, other days just one thing. And it's okay if it's the same thing that I've written the day before, and the day before that. Often, I want to shout, 'I'm not frigging grateful for anything!', but I force myself to look at my lists and I see that I've found things the days before, so I can do it again that day.

Recognising what you're grateful for isn't an all-purpose antibiotic for depression. Making a list each day won't make your illness disappear. The seas don't part and make you realise that depression doesn't matter because you have a healthy spider plant.

Imagine a hot curry full of beautifully blended and complementary spices that make it absolutely delicious. Flavours are pinging around your taste buds. Then depression comes along and takes away the turmeric and the coriander and the ginger and the black pepper and the cardamom and the cumin, and leaves you with nothing. Gratitude is the process of getting some of those spices back in. It puts some of the hope and vitality back that depression takes. It helps contradict depression when it says, 'You have nothing; you are nothing.'

And remember to thank Pluto.

32. Medicate! Medicate!

Citalopram! Escitalopram! Fluoxetine! Sertraline!
Lithium! Venlafaxine! Imipramine! Mirtazapine!
Quetiapine! Come on down!

These are all the drugs I have been prescribed. I'm
still taking escitalopram. Big up for escitalopram in the
house! Woo!

Sorry, I'll stop now.

At some point you will need to think about anti-
depressants. If you get prescribed them, a doctor will
be involved, and if you're lucky, they will tell you about
all the side effects. If your doctor doesn't mention side
effects at all, go and see another doctor, seriously.
Side effects are the most important aspect of anti-
depressants to talk about. You will also need to talk
about how long it will take the medication to work,
the dosage you're being put on and when you need to
come back, but knowing about side effects trumps all
of those.

Here's me back at the doctors after a few weeks on anti-depressants for the first time:

DOCTOR: How are you feeling?

ME: Mood is a bit better. I feel pretty dizzy though.

DOCTOR: Right.

ME: And sick.

DOCTOR: Anything else?

ME: Really sleepy.

DOCTOR: Yes.

ME: My appetite has gone crazy.

DOCTOR: Okay.

ME: And, ummm, well, things are a bit, errr . . . a bit weird down, well, down there. I haven't been able to, well, you know . . . I haven't been . . . you know. You know?

DOCTOR: Sorry. What?

ME: I mean, the flagpole goes up, mostly, but it doesn't . . .

DOCTOR: Doesn't?

ME: It doesn't . . .well, it doesn't release its flag. At the end of the flag ceremony.

DOCTOR: What flag ceremony? Is this a musculoskele-tal thing? Are you in the scouts?

ME: No, listen. Okay, us gentlemen have flagpoles, right?

DOCTOR: Right.

ME: And sometimes, the flagpole goes up but at the end of the 'ceremony', at the point of the 'release' of the flag, it doesn't always . . . come out and flap in the wind.

DOCTOR: Oh. Oh, yes. I see, yes. Oh, okay.

ME: Maybe I have a weird virus of some sort?

DOCTOR: No, I don't think so. These are all common side effects from the anti-depressants you're taking.

ME: They're what?

DOCTOR: Common side effects, happen to most people. Well, for men who have a flagpole, obviously.

ME: They're side effects? All of them?

DOCTOR: Yes.

ME: But, you didn't mention this might happen.

DOCTOR: Didn't I? Oh well, they don't happen to everyone. Just some people. Well, a lot of people. Most people.

ME: But – but . . . Why didn't you tell me? I mean, you never mentioned it.

DOCTOR: Oh well, you know now, don't you?

ME: (*Gets up out of chair. Exits stage left, slamming door dramatically, like the end scene in a bad soap opera. Cue music.*)

After that incident, I make sure I always ask about side effects. I've also became less tolerant of doctors saying, 'See if the side effects go away after a few weeks.' Sod that. When you've been falling off your bike due to dizziness, falling asleep at 10 a.m. and almost falling down the loo from being sick, you start wondering if the positive effects really outweigh the negative side effects.

These days, if I have side effects that I can't tolerate after a decent amount of time, I insist on trying something else. There are lots of different medications. The holy grail of anti-depressants is obviously a medication without any nasty side effects that still dramatically improves your mood.

Also don't be afraid to go back to your doctor if you feel the medication has stopped working. A lot of medications I've taken have worked well for a year or so and then stopped, so I've gone back and tried something else. With medications it's not as simple as being put on one type and then that's it for the foreseeable future. It's an ongoing process of experimenting and evaluating what works the best. Don't settle for something that's not working for you, all right? If your doctor or psychiatrist challenges this, just say, 'James told me to.'

If you ever get to a point when you want to reduce the amount of anti-depressants you're on, or come off altogether, then this needs to be done very carefully as the side effects can be hard to manage. Again, you have to do this with a doctor. And, again, get a good one who will talk to you comprehensively about what might happen and keep checking on how you're doing to make sure you're not reducing too fast.

Finally, a word about people who 'pill shame', who make comments about the dangers of anti-depressants, or how they're unnecessary, or if you were really strong you wouldn't need them. There are lots of comebacks you can give these people, including: 'If I had high blood pressure, would you be judging me for taking medication?' Or 'These pills help me stay alive. I'm happy to stop taking them if you're happy to take the responsibility for my death.' Or, possibly my favourite, complete with an enormous eye roll, 'Oh, just sod off.'

Pill shaming often comes from people who have never had depression themselves, but are happy to tell you that kiwano fruit is nature's anti-depressant and ask why you aren't eating that, combined with a diet of lightly grilled soursop, because that's what works for them and they've never had depression.

For the record, it's fine to take anti-depressants – they may even save your life – but get informed, and talk about the side effects with a decent doctor.

Here endeth the lecture.

33. Rest

Take a seat. A really large comfy one with those cool
extendable footrests. One that feels snuggly and warm and
you can curl up in.

Depression is major trauma to your body, mind and
spirit, so you have to rest because your soul needs to heal;
depression impacts on the very essence of who you are.

Depression, in all its forms, is a nasty piece of work,
and it is powerful. Don't underestimate its impact. I had
to change my life radically in order to manage it, and at
the time it really sucked. I really resented it, I still resent
it, but I know depression isn't going anywhere, so I have
to work alongside it, keep checking on how I'm doing and
make the necessary changes. Admittedly, I'd rather it
just buggered off and haunted one of my enemies (Shane
Rowan from secondary school, I mean you), but it's not
going to do that. It lessens; it gets better; life becomes more
manageable. But for me, and many others, it doesn't leave
altogether.

I was fortunate to be able to take a whole year out. I left my job, and my full-time work became staying alive and managing depression. Taking time out isn't possible for everyone to do, especially if you have a mortgage the size of the CN Tower and fifteen guinea pigs to feed. But you have to create rest within your life. Remember you're ill; if you had any other life-threatening illness, you and everyone else around you would be certain you needed a break

and create the space for you to do this.

Resting gives you time to recover from the impact of depression and the daily thumping it gives you. Unless you stop and give yourself time to recuperate, depression will kick your arse. This might mean making major changes to your life, but it might also include sitting on the sofa more, watching trashy television, so there's a silver lining in everything, eh? It might mean being by yourself for a day, going for a coffee without your phone and watching the world go by. It might mean heading out to the countryside and watching the wind blow a field of grass in all directions – beautiful, right?

You have to treat depression seriously because your life is at risk. This illness routinely and carelessly kills people because the pain is too much. If you run a multi-million pound business where you get up at 5 a.m. and don't leave work until 9 p.m., then please take a good look at what could happen if you don't make changes in your life. And also please lend me a fiver.

You can't outrun depression. Trust me, I tried. I saw the signs, I felt the weight of it inside me, but I thought I could carry on and it would go away. I tried running by ignoring it, by being busy, by convincing myself it wasn't behind me and just by keeping going. You can never run fast enough. Depression caught up with me and clubbed me over the head like a starving, sprinting Neanderthal. When depression has been chasing you, and finally catches you, it's worse because it's frigging furious and is out for revenge.

Grab rest whenever and however you can. In fact, stop reading this and rest.

34. Slides and ladders

You're going down a huge dark slide. It's slippy and terrifying. You try to stop yourself falling further down, but it's too late; you're falling, and you can't stop.

This slide is suicide. You won't find it in your local theme park – that would frankly be dangerous and a little inappropriate. (For the record, I really like slides. I mean, not this particular slide, but in general slides are the best thing in parks. Don't stop going on slides: they'll feel hurt and I'll feel guilty.)

Depression pushes us down the suicide slide, and once we've started down the slide, it greases the slide so we go down even faster. In other words, it's easy to get triggered to think about suicide once those feelings have started. And the lure of suicide can be very strong; it's like trying to keep awake in a dark cinema, watching a boring afternoon film on a hot day when you've only slept for three hours the night before.

Sometimes people hit the bottom of the slide and

survive; sometimes people don't. But once the slide has come into your life, it's always there. There is always a risk you can start to fall down.

Many seemingly trivial things can trigger my suicidal thoughts: looking in a full-length mirror, hearing music through someone else's earphones on a train, seeing the picture of a neglected animal, a stressful day at work, ripping my favourite trousers, people chewing gum with their mouths open. Irritation moves to anger, moves to shame, moves to self-hatred, moves to lack of hope and finally moves to suicidal thoughts and the slide. Other times there is no trigger; it just arrives and I'm sliding down.

Anyhoo, you know that slide? Well, what you didn't know is that there is a ladder right beside it. It's in the dark too so you have to reach out to feel it. You have to remember, and preferably write down, what can help you reach the ladder. Oh, and depression will convince you that there is no ladder and that you're much better falling all the way down. But we know depression is as reliable as scaffolding made of jelly. Trust me, there is a ladder – I don't lie, and depression does.

I have different ways of reaching the ladder. Usually I have to go to sleep with a sleeping pill and mute out the pain until it passes. Other times I send a text to a crisis helpline, so I can tell someone that I'm feeling suicidal, and that helps. Other times I just have to get out, get some fresh air and punch an old lady. Okay, I don't punch old ladies. Even if it helped, I wouldn't do that. Well, probably not.

Sometimes I sit on the sofa, rocking, holding my aching head, and I repeat, 'This will get better, this will get better, this will get better.' The moment-by-moment approach (see Chapter 20) works here too – not to immediately get rid of the suicidal thoughts, but to keep me alive so that if I can get through this immediate moment, and then the next, the thoughts will eventually subside. You can prove to yourself that you're getting through this.

My biggest tool for surviving suicidal thoughts is waiting. Whilst I wait, I think a lot about change, and how change is inevitable. I think how the clouds keep moving over my head. I think about the different headlines that will be in the papers tomorrow; how people will get married and divorced, get different jobs; how dogs will have puppies; how birds will migrate; and how the tides will be different tomorrow too. Change means that my thoughts will change, and I won't be like this forever.

I also look at my file of photos titled 'Moments of Joy'. I look at the pictures and make myself remember that I've had suicidal feelings before, that they've always gone, and then I've been able to experience these very moments. A delicious lemon ice cream, seeing a lavish Hindu wedding in India, having pancakes and vodka in St Petersburg, the warm sun on my legs one morning whilst reading a book, seeing a heron take flight, a tree in bright yellow glory in Autumn, a boozy picnic in a park with friends, a funny play that had me in stitches and cherry blossom chasing me down the street.

It's whatever works, folks; whatever works for you. Maybe create a safe space in your mind, and head there for some peace. Do what you can do to get through.

35. Finding the point in 'What's the bloody point?'

'Raindrops on roses, and whiskers on kittens' don't give me meaning in my life. I hate roses with their 'Ooh look at me, look how lovely I am' and then they pierce your flesh without a thought. Kittens' whiskers are insignificant; bright copper kettles leak; warm woollen mittens have been on the radiator too long and will give you second-degree burns.

With depression you feel awful. Then you feel awful about feeling awful. Then you feel awful for other people having to put up with your awfulness. Then you wish that you could never feel awful again but then you feel awful as you know you *will* feel awful again.

When depression is stripping us of who we are, isolating us from those we love and convincing us that we're worthless, it's understandable that we struggle to find meaning in our lives. It's easy and logical to get to a stage when you think, 'Why bother any more? What's the point?'

Recovery is about finding meaning. Without meaning in our lives we don't fully live. Finding meaning in your life is linked to how you see yourself as a person, what your identity is. With all the losses that depression brings, it can be hard to understand who you are now. You need to spend time considering what can bring you fulfilment and add the meaning that depression has taken away.

I knew that I couldn't go back to the job I had before I was ill. It was too stressful and required too much energy. Therefore I had to look for something that would fulfil me but that I could manage with depression in tow. Sadly, there weren't many jobs where you could get paid to lie on the sofa with your cat, eating toast, but I found a job in a library, which I love. It gives me meaning because I love books, I love people (well, some of them) and I love being part of the community. Each time I put on my lanyard, I think, 'Yes, this is a big part of who I am. I'm James, who works in a library' and that thought gives two fingers to depression, who told me I could never live, let alone work again.

A bit like discovering the right hobby, you also have to find time to see what can add meaning for you. It could be a different job, one that connects to you and your values. I'm a great believer in finding a job that you actively look forward to. Once, when I was complaining to a friend about one of my first jobs after leaving university – I was cleaning toilets in a hospital – and he said, 'But you're not supposed to like your job; no one does.' This couldn't be further from the truth. You *are* supposed to like your job. In fact, it's really important that you do because you could be spending more than thirty-five hours a week there. Would you recommend a friend do something they hated for that many hours?

Of course, meaning doesn't have to be found through work; there are other things that can give you purpose. Think about what you're good at, or what you were passionate about before depression started to squash you. Perhaps there's a charitable cause you care about? Have you always wanted to learn an instrument? Take evening classes? How about spirituality or religion? It doesn't matter – what matters is that it connects to the part of you that cares. When you feel strongly about something, or get angry at an injustice, or feel something that brings a flutter inside you, that's what you should try to do. Just remember my words in Chapter 29 and don't take on a project that involves too much stress. We are talking light pursuits that will bring you joy and pleasure.

Now, go sign up for those Belarusian samba classes.

36. Start sharing

Someone once sat next to me in a group therapy session,
took my hand in theirs, smiled with condescension, and
said, 'Listen, James, if you care, you'll share.' I nearly
vomited with the amount of saccharine liberally sprinkled
on to their words. But, annoyingly, it got me thinking.

What would happen if I shared my experience of depression with others? How would people react? Would they
make remarks that would make me feel worse? But so what
if they did? It seemed risky but appealing at the same time.

I sat down on my bed with my tiny white laptop and
started to write about depression, what it had done to me,
what I felt, what I was still feeling and how I hated depression. I did a few different drafts and I felt good for writing
about it. I could have left it there, alone on my laptop, but I
took a chance and I put it out into the world on a blog and
promoted it on social media. After ten months, a grand
total of three people had read it. But those three people all
made comments and said they liked it and that it helped

them. They understood all the strange pain, the lack of hope, the way you could never fully explain to other people what depression felt like. They got it and I loved them for it.

I think of those three people as my own original gang members. It was great to be part of a gang, my very own posse. My gang! I had never been in a proper gang. They didn't know they were in my gang, obviously, but still, they were my depression gang! We could give ourselves ridiculous nicknames, invent a special language and design our own graffiti tag.

Isolation is dangerous, especially with depression. By sharing our stories with fellow depressionites, it rings a bell; our experience chimes in with others and we meet each other at the place of shared compassion and recognition. When you share your pain and connect with others, something really beautiful happens.

Social media is responsible for a lot of utter tosh, stupid bickering and time-wasting, but when I was first unwell, it helped me massively. I would post tweets of how I was feeling, what I was scared about and what I had accomplished that day, in spite of depression. Comments like 'I feel that too' or 'It really sucks, doesn't it?' or 'Well done!' reached out to me and touched the parts that were in the most pain. Even one or two 'likes' or seeing that people had read the post really helped. I started to feel less shame because other people validated what I was feeling, and I could see that there were many others in the same situation. I couldn't be that weird if all these other people had similar feelings, could I?

There are plenty of ways to share your story, but a blog is a great one to start with, as you can remain anonymous if you want to and you can disable comments if you're not ready for that. Or maybe you could volunteer for your local mental health charity, who are often looking for stories to inspire and support others. Maybe you can attend a depression support group and tell your tale, or write an article for a local paper.

Sharing became slightly infectious for me. I told everyone, thankfully nearly always with a positive reaction. But in truth, the train conductor didn't need to know I had depression, nor did the street cleaner, nor the vet or the nice man stacking tins of spaghetti hoops at the supermarket.

At the post office counter:

ME: Can I have three second-class stamps please?

WOMAN: Of course.

ME: Thank you. Stamps are really beautiful, aren't they?

WOMAN: Umm, yes. I suppose so.

ME: It's just that I have depression, and sometimes it's hard to see beauty.

WOMAN: Right. Yes. Okay.

ME: Thank you. I'm going to write some letters, that helps my depression too.

WOMAN: (*Frantically presses the button as I'm still standing at the counter.*) Cashier number three please.

I needed to tell people. It did me good because I was saying to others and depression itself, 'I'm not going to keep this secret. I'm not a pariah; I'm not ashamed.'

Sharing chips away at depression's wall because it wants you to feel worthless and alone. The point is that you share, you open up and you say to the world, 'This is my story. This is how it is for me. Now tell me about you.'

We get through depression with each other, one sufferer to another.

37. Download some hope

Depression consumes your hope, eats it up, burps it out
with a loud *blerrruuuuuugh* and then goes back for more.
What's left is you feeling like a dark shell, devoid of all
vitality, with no sense of anything ever getting better.

But hope is the antidote to depression. It's the anti-
venom to the snake bite. So the trick is to find some, hang
on to it and not let depression touch it. Because it's going
to try to steal it from you without any shame, not caring
about you and desperate to fill its own stomach.

Hope comes in many forms, so there's a lot of choice,
but you have to choose carefully; it can't be something that
could collapse easily. So banking on your football team
winning the FA Cup to keep you going isn't going to work
– especially if they're in the same league as the London
Metropolitan Police, which my local team is. You can't
go with fantasy stuff either; so hope in the form of a dark,
handsome soldier from ye olden times who will come on a
white steed to gallop you off into the sunset doesn't cut it,

and let's face it, do you know how to ride a horse anyway? Finally, if you're hoping for a mermaid/merman fantasy: see Chapter 20 – they're totally unreliable.

Anything uncertain, fragile and unrealistic doesn't work. You've got to play the odds here and make it a robust choice. If your only hope is to climb K2 within the next month, with no climbing experience, a fear of heights, a fear of mountains and a fear of flying to foreign countries, then depression is going to steal that one really easily.

Hope can seem small to the untrained eye, and it's not always the obvious things that come to mind. Petting a cat that accepts your love is hope, feeling well enough to thank the bus driver at the end of a journey is hope, smiling unexpectedly at a YouTube video of a panda going down a slide is hope. Hope can come in being greeted 'Good morning' by a stranger on the way to work, or a nice smile from the supermarket cashier that you always go to. A dog that licks your ears is hope; a plant that flowers despite you hacking it down because you thought it was an invasive Mexican weed is hope. It can be a cake that doesn't sink in the oven, or does sink in the oven but you put some cream and strawberries on top and pass it off as a triumph because it's yummy. Hope is also sending a photo of the collapsed cake to your WhatsApp group because they will tease you mercilessly, and that means they love you.

I have a hope list that I'm working slowly toward that

is realistic, meaningful and achievable, which feels good. Do steal from my list if you want to, but it's best to do your own. Here it is in its current form:

- Doing a really big belly laugh – the kind when you can't stop laughing, tears are coming out and your breath goes all weird.
- Smiling at a nice flower. Forgive this sounding like a hippy meme, but for ages seeing any beauty made no impact on me and I wanted that back, so it's on the list.
- Being able to sit through a film at the cinema without wanting to shout at the audience for eating sweets or wanting to run out of the building screaming at the hell of being in public with other people.
- Finishing a whole book and enjoying it.
- Being able to go on holiday, have a drink, enjoy the nice surroundings and not immediately feel the need to fly back home and make a den under my duvet and never come out.
- Being in a gallery and seeing a new painting that takes my breath away.
- Having at least one day a week when I giggle and feel childish.

Sometimes, hope arrives in unexpected ways, which is a real gift. Please write these down too. I call this my 'unexpected hope list' and write them on my memo pad on my phone so I can look at them when depression is wanting to feed. They include:

- Seeing a little girl unashamedly dressed as a pink hippopotamus, eating a hamburger in a café.
- Watching an older couple slowly dance on a bandstand.
- Seeing a nurse gently stroke the forehead of an ill patient.
- A grandfather reading a story to his grandchild and doing all the funny voices of the characters.
- Seeing a little dog carrying a stick four times the size of it, grinning with unabashed glee, accompanied by its mortified owner.

It's not that the moment of joy itself will miraculously cure depression (although it will really help for an hour or so), but the evidence that you *can* feel joy again really helps to erode it.

As time passes, I'll add to the lists, and it will give me a bank of hope, a large shield to repel depression.

153

38. Get better painkillers and do mindfulness your way

The pain of depression is all-encompassing. It's a type of pain that seems to emanate from our very core and invade us with speed and power. It can be paralysing, reducing us to a husk of our former selves. Someone once asked me to accurately describe the pain of depression. I couldn't. It was impossible; it's a pain that you can only understand if you've felt it.

My depression pain can hit me suddenly like a spade across the face. Or grow steadily over a number of days, like a poisonous rash. My instinct is to reach for a hammer and knock it into the side of my head. Please don't try this at home; it will hurt, and then you'll have double the pain and a dirty hammer. At home my hammer is hidden to stop me doing this, which is the right thing to do but makes it really hard when you have to put a nail into the wall with a can of reduced-sugar baked beans. The result is that I stay alive but all the paintings in our flat are wonky.

We have to find painkillers that work on depression, and I ain't talking a couple of paracetamol here. So what are the options?

Mindfulness meditation is hailed as a tonic by many. I'm going to be honest, it doesn't really work for me. I really tried, honestly, I did. (*Kneels on the floor, pleading in a praying position.*) Please don't hate me. I did a twelve-week intensive course, I practised every day for nine months, I read mindfulness meditation books, I listened to mindfulness meditation apps and watched mindfulness meditation videos. In short, I did my homework and all that happened was that I had more time to think about how crap depression was.

The problem with mindfulness meditation is that we often think we're not doing it right, or we have associations that act as barriers. We don't feel Zen enough, or we don't have any clean Buddhist monk robes in the wardrobe. We're uncomfortable on the cushion with our legs behind our neck, and all we can think about is the fact that the washing is on the line and it's raining.

On the course I did, I kept thinking I should be having revelatory spiritual thoughts but my mind either went to very dark places or I started wondering about the instructor. What did she have for breakfast? Where did she buy her trousers? Did she have a new washer/dryer or a cream carpet in their living room? What colour was her underwear? I was convinced all the other participants were on a better spiritual plane and I was left thinking about death and lino flooring.

Then, everyone else I knew with depression kept going on about how helpful mindfulness was to them, what a miracle it had been, how it had saved them. They were now off all their anti-depressants, running marathons (mindfully, obviously) and had never been happier. They were also eating mindfully, walking mindfully, colouring mindfully, gardening mindfully and, for all I knew, killing slugs mindfully. They had all reached level thirty-five on the 'nirvana scale of better people than me'.

Seriously pissed off, I gave up on my regular half an hour daily session of mindfulness meditation. I had tried too hard and it wasn't the right time or the right approach for me. Instead I opted for a simpler, quicker approach to mindfulness that didn't give depression an opportunity to come into my head. If I go for a walk, I look at a nice tree and really look at it, to the extent that if it were a person they would be massively offended. The same way young babies can stare at you without any compunction. I take a breath, stay in the moment and focus on my breathing. That's it. That's all I do. Then I might go to an art gallery and notice the brush marks on a painting, I take a breath and stay in that moment too. It's mindfulness in moments. If I still get thoughts like 'Why does Winnie-the-Pooh wear a jumper but no trousers?' then I leave the mind-fulness for a while and try to not give myself a hard time about it not working. For a little while it helps me stay in the present and not focus on the pain because my mind is going, 'Oh look, that bit of branch on that tree with the knobbles looks like a young Queen Victoria in profile.' You can even do the washing up mindfully – trickier if you have a dishwasher, obviously, but you get the point. Give it a go. If it's a tool that helps you, even in a small way, then it's worth a try, eh?

What else works? Well, podcasts work well for me. Try something funny if possible and play it through ear-phones to submerge yourself, distract you and counteract the pain in your head. Or play music, but you've got to be really, really careful what you listen to. Depression's playlist includes that top ten hit 'Everything is Terrible and I'm a Disgusting Person' – the melody to that one is cracking. And of course the famous, 'I'm in Pain and Feel So Much Shame'. We all know that one, don't we? Equally problematic is if you have something ridiculously opti-mistic like 'The World is a Wonderful Golden Place and I Love Everyone, La La La', that hit the Ibiza beaches in the 1990s, if I remember. Because, when you turn it off and return to the real world, the contrast can be pretty awful. Try something with a thumping beat (I know, I sound like your great grandfather), something that will tackle the pounding you're taking, and pound back with music. Or go the soothing route; that can work too. It doesn't need to be soothing lullabies sung by South Pacific blue whales – just something that calms you and lets you breathe.

Getting out into some kind of nature helps. I don't really know why, but it does. Head to the sea, some hills, a forest or a lake. A park doesn't cut it and nor does sitting by a duck pond; you need something much greater than yourself to shrink the pain. You don't need to do anything extreme like hike up a mountain, sleep without a tent amongst some sheep poo and eat nettles. Just spend a few hours wandering around, sitting and taking some deep breaths. The countryside has to be big, so think big hills (also known as mountains), big seas, big rivers, big forests, etc. When you see yourself in relation to an expanse of beauty it has a calming effect. If you don't get attacked by a snake, a bear or a golden eagle, then consider it a worthwhile trip.

Try moving your body. In any way that you can. Walk, run, skip, cycle, jog – hey, even get on a passing mule. The act of moving unsticks you from the pain. Sometimes I sit with my head throbbing and think, 'I can't get up, the pain is paralysing me,' but if I force myself to walk to the sea or to the shops or get on my bike, somehow the pain starts to shift.

Hit things. Not people. Anything else though. Okay, actually not animals, that's not allowed. I suppose you can't hit other people's cars either. Cushions love to be hit, so that will definitely work, and punch bags get offended if you don't hit them, so that's an obvious choice. You can hit water too, or foam, sand – all that kind of stuff works excellently.

Experiment with what works for you. When the emotional pain is starting to build, try things out and see what helps. If carving faces out of courgettes works (yes, this is a thing), then do it and don't judge it. Make some home-made pasta, build that model railway. As we know, depression will be telling you nothing will work, so ignore what's it's saying and try some new stuff.

159

39. Darken your humour (mwah ha ha)

A light-hearted, frivolous conversation with my husband:

ME: I feel like killing myself.

HIM: Oh, for goodness sake, not again. Well, don't use the washing line to hang yourself with because it's a bugger to get back up again and I have no clean pants.

ME: Okay.

HIM: And don't kill yourself anywhere I like to visit, or I'll resent you even more than I do already.

ME: Right. (*Silence.*) I'm a useless, horrible person.

HIM: And you're only realising this *now*? Blimey, I knew that when we first met.

ME: I'll never get any better.

HIM: Well, if you're not going to improve, think how that's going to be for *me,* seeing you wallow around the house emanating slime of self-pity. It's all 'me, me, me' with this depression thing.

ME: Stop. This is serious. (*I'm smiling a little.*)

HIM: It's not like I married you for your *joie de vivre* and sparkling personality.

ME: Oh, bugger off.

HIM: Or your money, or your good looks, or your career prospects, or your fashion sense.

ME: You're a pig.

HIM: Or your values, or your integrity, or your compassion, or your treatment of others.

ME: Stop it, you git.

HIM: Or your dance moves, or your ability to play chess, or your wisdom.

And then I'm smiling more now, laughing a little.

ME: I hate feeling like this.

HIM: I know. I know you do.

Then I start to see how absurd depression can sound and I can hear its ridiculous voice, which is firm and scary, but utterly, utterly, utterly stupid.

Darkening your humour shines a bright torch in depression's face. It's basically the Hercule Poirot of coping tools. Please put on a bad Belgian accent for this bit:

'I see you. I know your ways, your lies, your nonsense. I see through you and I know you're responsible. I accuse YOU.'

These days, when I feel horrendous, I instigate a conversation with my husband with dark humour. But you don't need someone else to help darken it; you can have the conversation with yourself, out loud if possible.

And the laughing helps too.

40. Take pride in staying alive

You're frigging awesome. Honestly, you are.   163

'I'm not.' I can hear you say, because that would be my
response as well. So let's look at the evidence.

**You're managing to stay alive when the illness
is routinely trying to take you down. You're getting
through each day whilst it's shouting at you, exhausting you and often trying to convince you to take your
own life. You're dying inside. It feels like you've been
robbed of your soul and you're still here. Sometimes
you're so ill you can't get out of bed, can't wash, can't
eat, can't concentrate, can't contact anyone, can't
sit still and can't feel anything. You feel unworthy,
washed up and defeated.**

Read the paragraph above again and notice that it
doesn't specify depression. Now pretend it's a friend
of yours talking about a physical illness they have.
What would be your response to how they're
managing it?

We don't feel pride in how we cope with depression because it's in our mind, and so we feel responsible for it. With mental illness, we think we should be able to feel better simply by pulling ourselves together because we equate it with feeling a little down.

It's so hard to remove the illness from ourselves, our identity, the essence of who we are, because it's in our brain. It's no wonder we struggle. If depression was in our ankles, it would still feel crap, but we'd be less hard on ourselves.

'Depression' isn't the right name for depression, if that makes sense. We need a new word not associated with sadness and not used frequently as an off-the-cuff adjective. What if we called it 'Tristitia Syndrome'? Then it would be so much easier to acknowledge our tenacity because it's not a common word in our vocabulary so it sounds removed from ourselves.

Read the above paragraph in bold again.

The fact that you're managing all of that is incredible.

The fact that you're here, reading this book, is incredible.

The fact that you've made it through to this very point now is incredible.

The case for the defence rests; you are officially awesome.

Now, let's all go tell depression to piss off.

Afterword

There was a time when illnesses of the mind were seen as demonic possession. And to anyone who has suffered from mental illness, including depression, there is a resonance that this term holds. There is some level of disconnection between who you feel you are and were, and the person looking back at you in the mirror, who seems vastly different and alien. Someone else wearing your clothes, sleeping your bed and steering your life.

Depression, and the experience of it, is a uniquely personal thing. But at the same time, it is one of the most common ailments of the modern age. And, curiously, it is one that's true nature can never really be captured in its entirety. We cannot share our minds, but try to communicate in stifled language a new self that seems so comprehensively unfamiliar that we would beg for just one moment of our lives before.

It is a condition that influences us all. Some of the greatest poetry, music and film has been written by those in its thrall, and we recognise within us the yearning that colours depression as if we have known it all along. And yet, when we join that thrall, we do not feel part of a collective, but abandoned by others to the very macabre oddness that we would celebrate as art. That is the great power of this demon, to be both so familiar and yet make us feel so different.

As both a psychiatrist and patient, the mechanism of depression seems to bring two worlds together. On one hand there is the science – neurological, biological or psychological – and on the other there is the subjective experience, the change in the portrait that comes undetected.

The two will often join, but rarely without hindsight as the illness fades. Thoughts that seemed so real and utterly convincing are suddenly brought to the light and shown to be what they are: symptoms of an illness. If only we could see this when under its power.

In my clinics I have seen people from all walks of life. Mostly, depression does not come without herald. In fact, most episodes of major mental illness come after a trauma, principally after a loss. It may not be immediately, but sometimes the external events of the world can open a door to something darker. And over time, this thing we call depression can begin to take us over. Or that is what it feels like.

Some suggest that it is an empathic creature, its designs benevolent and fashioned to protect you from the harsh realities of existence. It comes to you as a warm darkness: one of exhaustion, where peace and silence are all that matters. We draw away into an internal world, a retreat from the pain. And depression tells us that this is good.

Others see it as malignant, callous and overpowering. A sudden wave of non-existence, cold and hard. The sharp corners of the world draw in until there is nowhere left to move. What was once bright and musical becomes dull and monotonous. Our urge to eat disappears, and we are left a zombie passing through a disinterested world, a punishment. And depression tells us that this is good.

For the poet, it is a rich tapestry from which to glean epithets, and for the scientist, a frustrating imp who eludes capture. But for the patient, it is all-encompassing. It is not a pathway to some great work, but feels like an early end to work unfinished. And once again, depression celebrates.

But it, like the rising and setting of the sun, is a natural phenomenon. It is part of our DNA, and as an extension, our psychological make-up. To deny its veracity is as fool-ish as it is to deny its transience. No matter what purpose it has, the effects are temporary, and it can be overcome. Humans have survived this long, and you are part of that

169

survival. The parts of you that make depression possible are just a tiny part of an incredible machine that is built to overcome it.

How we do so is very much up to us, and that is where its power falters. Depression is not a choice, but to continue living, to fight back and reclaim yourself is. And you can.

The fight has taken many forms over time. Freud and the neo-Freudians championed the role of unconscious influence on our perceptions, where the unknown beneath our cognition ruled our life like Gods. Therapy was designed to witness their movements, to gain their intention and to subvert melancholy through self-reflection.

Later came an age of medicine, where pills targeting complex hierarchies of hormones and transmitters were the mainstay of treatment. In between came great advances of self-empowerment, such as cognitive therapies, teaching us to heal ourselves.

Today, we realise that depression (amongst other mental illness) is not as simple as to have one cause. Yes, there may be a trauma, but genetics play a role. A pill may work for one, but therapy for another. Depression is not one demon, but something without constant form that shifts to fit us. And with that, its weaknesses differ too. And finally, we are talking about it openly. No demon can survive all of us.

In my experience, there are many qualities that my patients who succeed in battling depression have (and I haven't met one personally yet who has not). The first is bravery in the face of adversity, a refusal to let the warm dark survive. The second is an acceptance of reality, and that they are not to blame for their suffering. A third, and this can be the hardest of all, is the wilful recognition of the need for help. These three things together, although part of a greater arsenal, seem to be what forms the basis of recovery.

Within each, there are certain truths which persist. Bravery is not as simple as winning, but to continue a fight when all seems lost. It is waking up in the morning, picking up the phone to dial a friend, choosing to question negative thoughts or reach for a coffee. Every little effort that fights back is a moment of bravery, just as every stroke against a tidal wave requires determination. Bravery, by definition, is defiance of the odds. And when you are depressed, those odds can seem very stacked indeed.

Acceptance of one's condition, without self-reproach or judgement, is another cornerstone. As humans living in a material world full of value judgements, the effects of depression can seem to place you as below others. If you are not working, or socialising, or eating, it is a curiosity that we blame ourselves for such punishment.

We would not exact this punishment on ourselves by

choice, or blame ourselves for such, but the depressed mind will try. Accepting that you are ill, and not that you are unworthy of happiness, can make all the difference. Blame is a trick played by the illness, and we will not fall for it.

The final key part is asking for help. In the same way that you would ask for a crutch for a broken leg (although a broken leg is much more simple), we need help to lift ourselves up. There is no shame in asking others for assistance, and it is brave to do so. It is a moment of realising that the illness will not win, and that you are not to blame, that you are worthy of receiving help, and then seeking it.

From reading the kind words in this book, it became very clear in the underlying message between the lines: Depression is something we can all experience, and it is human. And it is in that shared humanity that we can help ourselves, and each other.

The chapters in this book address the various comic forms that depression will take. They address the lies it will whisper in your ear, and the habits you will use to drown them out. They offer simple advice on living, to allow us to rediscover what was once the norm. Crucially, they see the humanity in illness, and propensity for our spirit to find coalescence in shared experience and will. As such, this book is not a dry academic tome, but a vivid and refreshingly real conversation.

Many of the chapters may seem strikingly familiar, others may seem weird and vague. But that's the demon: a shape-shifter. But if you are reading this book, then life has drawn you to this place where the stories are likely to share words with your own. You are not alone. And although the language may appear to only scratch the surface of your experience, it is nice to know that someone sees you down there in the dark and is ready to plunge in after you.

173

It is together that we rise back up. It is together that we rediscover ourselves. We recognise that the alien in the mirror is us, and that the illusion can be broken. Crucially, we learn that we are not alone in our fight, and that the commonality of depression is its greatest weakness. We are alive together, and the stories are shared.

So, in parting, I will say this. You have already shown bravery. You have already shown acceptance. And you have already taken a step to seek help. We could not ask anything more of ourselves or others, and that call will be answered. Depression, demon or not, is not forever. And each step forward is one closer to recovery.

And, one day, you can say with utter conviction that the future can be taken back.

Dr Ben Janaway, psychiatrist and writer